CONTENTS

DISCOVERING PHOTOSHOP

WITH THE HELP OF SOFTWARE LIKE PHOTOSHOP, THE WORLD OF PHOTOGRAPHY NOW EXTENDS MUCH FURTHER THAN JUST TAKING PICTURES...

Digital photography has well and truly revolutionised the way we take pictures. It's now possible to see your photos on a camera's screen in an instant and record hundreds of pictures on a single memory card. Modern digital cameras now completely outshine their film cousins in terms of power, and each new launch seems to boast higher resolutions with accompanying detailed, well-exposed pictures. But anyone who thinks that digital photography is just about cameras and taking photos is missing out on a whole world of fun.

Software like Adobe Photoshop and its 'lite' more affordable counterpart, Adobe Photoshop Elements, allows you to explore digital further than simply capturing a scene with your camera. This software lets you manipulate the pixels that make up your digital images and control the results, too.

The concept of post-processing isn't strictly new - it's just like hand printing from a negative but working with digital files is so much easier than using the old enlargers and smelly chemicals in a darkroom, and gives you infinitely more creative

possibilities. This book is testament to that - the digital darkroom is at your disposal and the only limit is your imagination. Photoshop makes all this extra creativity easy and has become the norm in the world of photography; so much so, you will get left behind if you don't join in! To 'Photoshop' an image has even become a verb in its own right!

Apart from revolutionising cameras, digital photography has given us more control over the whole process of taking and making pictures - you take a picture, improve it or add creative effects, then print out or share the results digitally with your friends and family - if this sounds good to you, then you've come to the right place! Everything you need to make great images is right here with our easy-to-follow techniques. So, let's get started...

DIGITAL PROVIDES THE PHOTOGRAPHER WITH INFINITELY MORE CREATIVE POSSIBILITIES

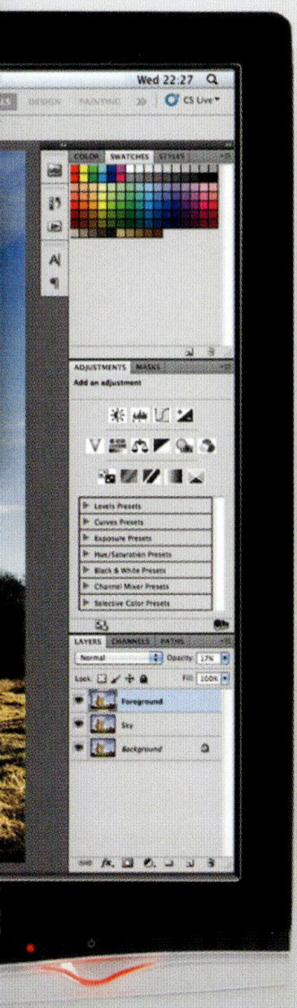

PRINT OUT YOUR IMAGE & SHOW OFF YOUR CREATION

When you've made your adjustments and are happy with your pictures, make sure you don't hide them away in a folder on your hard drive! Why not show them off in a print or in an online gallery like the one on our website *www.photoanswers.co.uk/gallery* - just follow the instructions to upload your images for all to see and enjoy!

UNDERSTANDING PHOTOSHOP

IMPROVE YOUR DIGITAL IMAGES WITH THE MENUS & PALETTES OF THE EDITING INTERFACE

IF THE SCREEN on the right looks scary to you, don't worry, we all have to start somewhere and anyone who says they weren't a bit confused the first time they sat down in front of Photoshop or Elements is a bare-faced liar! Just like any new technology you encounter, it will take some time to get used to, but this overview should certainly help. Individual windows and palettes can be shifted from one side to the other and moved around just like a regular Windows display. But if you want something a bit more ordered, they can also be locked in place at the sides of the screen. Click and drag the Toolbox to the edge of the screen and you'll see this happen.

Whatever you choose, don't be afraid to experiment – the interface won't break just because you move a few windows around and if you lose anything, just go to the *Window* menu and pick *Reset Palette Locations*. If you're looking at a more streamlined display than the one opposite, click on the *Edit* tab top-right and then select *Full* instead of *Quick* or *Guided*.

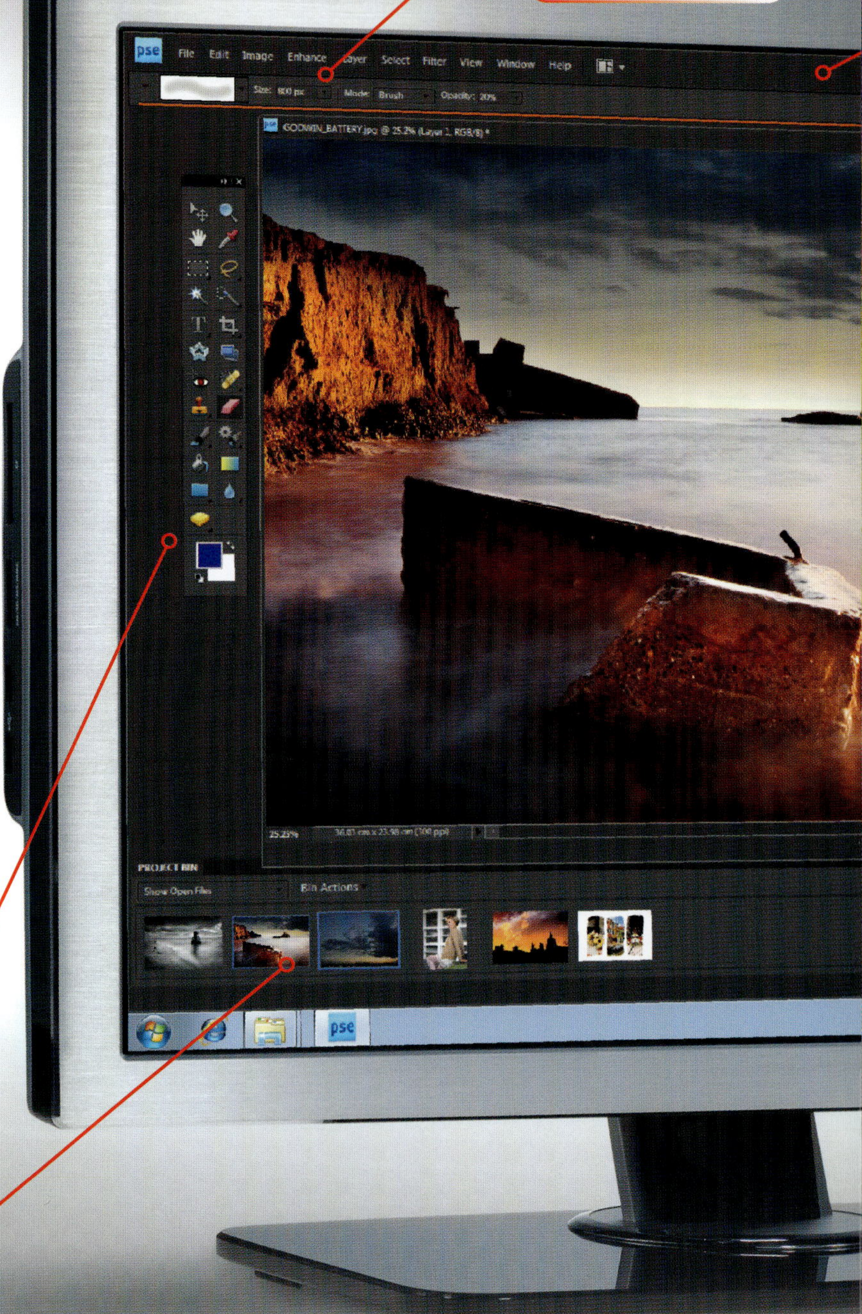

OPTIONS BAR
The options here change depending on which tool you have selected in the Toolbox. Selecting the *Eraser tool*, for example, will bring up options to change its size, shape, opacity and more.

TOOLBOX
This contains shortcuts to many of the major tools you need for image editing, including those that control Selections, Cropping and Cloning. Tools are activated by a single click of the mouse and remain active until another tool is selected (for more on the Toolbox, see page 8).

THE PHOTO BIN (ELEMENTS ONLY)
All the images you currently have open will be displayed in here. This makes it easy to swap between them at will. You can also right-click on any of the thumbnails to access handy information about the image, rotate or duplicate it.

WINDOWS & PALETTES CAN BE MOVED AROUND JUST LIKE IN A REGULAR WINDOWS DISPLAY, SO THERE'S NOTHING TO FEAR!

TOP TIP
For a better look at your image, hide all the palettes on screen by pressing the *Tab* key. To bring them back, just press *Tab* again.

MENU BAR
Gives access to a multitude of options - everything from opening and closing pictures with the *File* menu, to changing its size, lighting and applying special filters. Just click on one of the options and a drop-down list will appear.

DISPLAY ICONS
If you're struggling to see two pictures on screen at the same time click the two small squares next to the minimise button or go to *Window→Images→Cascade* or *Tile*.

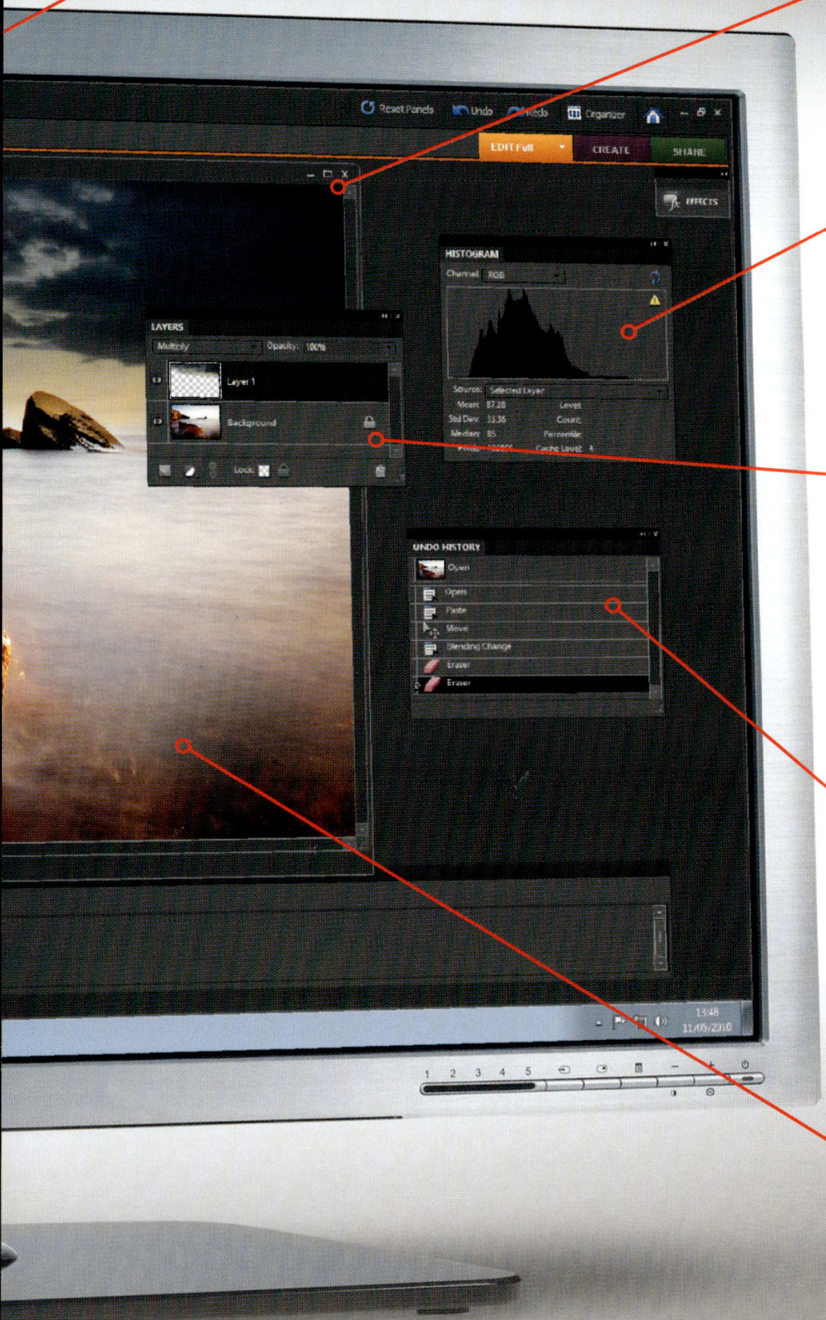

HISTOGRAM
Gives a 'live' graph, showing how light and dark pixels are distributed throughout the image. This will change as you make adjustments and the Histogram also responds to any Selections you've made and which Layer you're on, showing the pixel values within the selected area.

LAYERS PALETTE
One of the most important palettes you'll ever use in Photoshop and Elements, this controls how the different Layers of the image interact with each other through Opacity, Adjustment Layers, Blending Modes, and Layer Masks (Photoshop only). JPEG files and converted RAWs will open with a single *Background* Layer, while Photoshop (.PSD) files and TIFFs can contain multiple Layers. To open the *Layers palette* press *F7* (Photoshop) or *F11* (Elements) or go to the *Window* menu and pick *Layers*.

UNDO HISTORY
The saviour of many a frustrated image-maker, the *Undo History* (*History palette* in Photoshop) allows you to 'step back' through the adjustments you've made. The amount of *History States* you can work back through depends on what you've set in the *Preferences* (*Edit→Preferences*). Just click on them to move back, a bit like pressing *Ctrl+Z* on the keyboard (or *Edit→Undo* in the menu).

IMAGE WINDOW
This displays the picture you're working on and any changes you make to it. The size your image is displayed (its magnification) can be changed by pressing *Ctrl* and the + or - keys on the keyboard, and you can zoom in to anything up to 3200%, depending on your version of Photoshop or Elements. However, most people find it comfortable to work on their images at 25% or so, only zooming in to make very fine alterations.

Various Guides, Grids and Rulers can be overlaid on your image to help composition or layout (go to the *View* menu for these) and in the full version of Photoshop you can press the *F* key to toggle between *Full Screen* mode and the regular view.

THE ELEMENTS TOOLBOX

PACKED WITH FEATURES, THE TOOLBOX IS YOUR FIRST STEP ON THE ROAD TO GREAT DIGITAL PICS...

THE TOOLBOX is perhaps your most important contact with Photoshop and Elements – it's your direct route to the real photo-editing power locked away inside your software. Therefore it's something that you need to be comfortable using if you want to start improving your pictures without a lot of head scratching.

Usually found floating to the side of the photo you're working on, the tools are accessed simply by clicking on them, but can also be activated through keyboard shortcuts (see the list on the right). If one of the tools has a small arrow next to it, just press and hold the mouse button for a flyout list of more options. Positions of the tools may vary from version to version, but their essential functions remain the same.

TOP TIP

Multiple tools can be accessed by the same key. To cycle through them, press the *Shift* key and the shortcut you want to use. *Shift+O*, for example, cycles through the *Dodge*, *Burn* and *Sponge* tools.

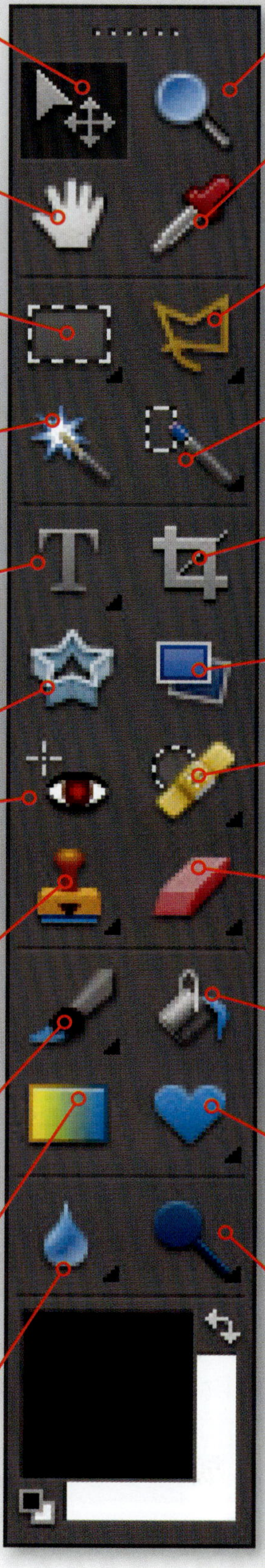

THE MOVE TOOL
Literally moves parts of the image around, can't be used on the *Background* Layer or you'll get a 'Locked pixels' warning.

THE HAND TOOL
Used to scroll around the image. This icon can be double-clicked to make an image fit on the screen.

THE MARQUEE TOOLS
Used to make broad Selections, usually covering a lot of pixels. Clicked and dragged over an image, these can be Rectangular or Elliptical.

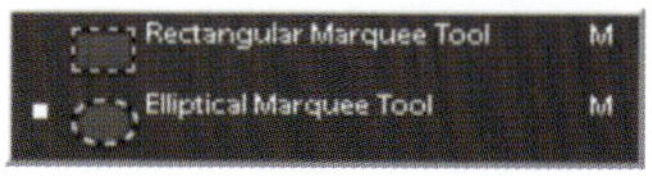

THE MAGIC WAND TOOL
Used to select lots of similarly coloured pixels, such as a clear blue sky. The accuracy is based on a given *Tolerance*, set in the Options bar.

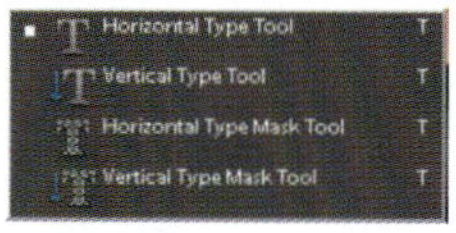

THE TYPE TOOL
Used to add text to your images. Selecting this and clicking on the image will create a new Type Layer onto which you can write.

RED-EYE REMOVAL TOOL
Drag this tool over any people with red-eye in your shot and it'll be quickly removed.

COOKIE CUTTER TOOL
Cuts preset shapes from your image using vector-based paths.

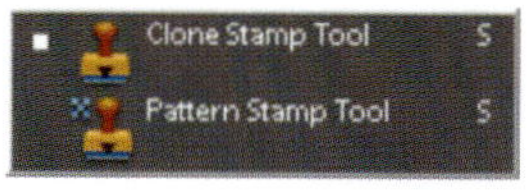

CLONE STAMP TOOL
Used to sample pixels from one part of the image and paint over another, removing distractions.

THE BRUSH TOOLS
Work just like a regular paintbrush, allowing you to paint onto your picture (or a Mask) like you would a real canvas. The *Brush tool* can be any size or shape you like.

THE GRADIENT TOOL
Lets you draw a gradient; very useful in conjunction with *Adjustment Layers* and *Layer Masks* (in Photoshop).

BLUR TOOL
Allows you to blur small, individual parts of the image by hand, using a brush. Also contains the *Sharpen* and *Smudge* tools which act in a similar way.

THE ZOOM TOOL

Allows you to click directly on the image to zoom in, or drag the tool over the exact area you want to magnify. Press and hold *Alt* to zoom out.

THE EYEDROPPER TOOL

Lets you sample colours directly from the image, just by clicking on it.

THE LASSO TOOL

Used to make finer, more accurate, Selections than the *Marquee* tools. The regular *Lasso tool* lets you draw over the pic like a pen, while the *Polygonal Lasso* offers a more precise, point-and-click approach.

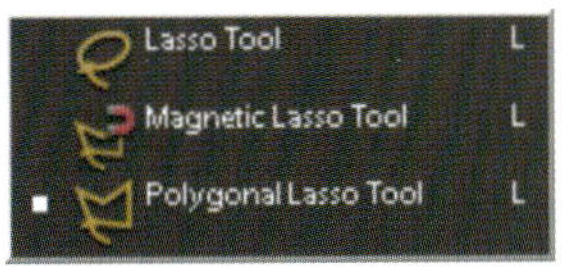

QUICK SELECTION TOOL

Allows you to paint a Selection using an adjustable brush. The Selection will expand as you drag following any defined edges in the image.

THE CROP TOOL

Allows you to trim images, cut out dead space, and resize them to whatever dimensions you like using presets in the Options bar.

STRAIGHTEN TOOL

Drag this tool out to follow the horizon in your image and the shot will be automatically straightened up.

HEALING BRUSH TOOL

Paint over any imperfections with these brushes to remove them. The *Spot Healing Brush tool* does this automatically, while the *Healing Brush tool* requires you to select pixels first, using the *Alt* key.

ERASER TOOL

Used to delete pixels from the image, the size of the *Eraser tool* can be controlled like a brush in the Options bar.

THE PAINT BUCKET TOOL

Lets you flood a chosen colour into an area of the image - this could be based on a Selection or on a *Tolerance* value.

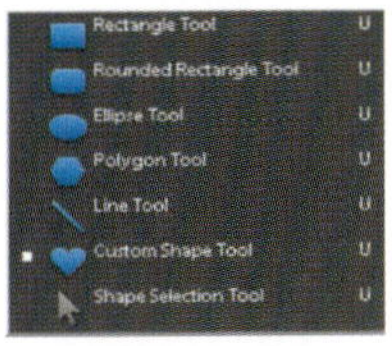

THE SHAPE TOOL

Allows you to quickly create a vast array of Vector shapes, which can be very useful for more graphical styles of work.

THE DODGE TOOL

Used to lighten parts of the image by hand and can be set to alter *Shadows*, *Midtones* or *Highlights* by various Exposures. Also accesses the *Burn* and *Sponge tools*, darkening and desaturating the image respectively.

CUT-OUT & KEEP
KEYSTROKE GUIDE

Speed up your digital workflow with these easy-to-use Toolbox shortcuts for Photoshop and Elements.

EDIT

Copy	**Ctrl+C**
Cut	**Ctrl+X**
Paste	**Ctrl+V**
Clear (a Selection)	**Backspace**
Free Transform	**Ctrl+T**
Undo	**Ctrl+Z**

LAYERS

Make a new Layer	**Ctrl+Shift+N**
Paste Layer/Selection to new Layer	**Ctrl+J**
Merge Layers	**Ctrl+E**
Merge all visible Layers	**Ctrl+Shift+E**
Control Layer Opacity (10-100%)	**Numeric keypad 1-0**

DISPLAY

Fit on screen	**Ctrl+0**
View at 100%	**Ctrl+Alt+0**
Zoom in / Zoom out	**Ctrl++ / Ctrl+ -**
Hide all palettes	**Tab**
Cycle to Full Screen mode *(PS only)*	**F**
Show/Hide Grid	**Ctrl+'**
Show/Hide Guides *(PS only)*	**Ctrl+;**

TOOLS

Brush tool	**B**
Crop tool	**C**
Set Default Colours	**D**
Eraser tool	**E**
Gradient/Paint Bucket tool	**G**
Hand tool (toggle)	**H (SPACEBAR)**
Lasso tool	**L**
Marquee tool	**M**
Dodge/Burn/Sponge tool	**O**
Clone Stamp tool	**S**
Move tool	**V**
Switch Colours	**X**
Zoom tool	**Z**
Increase / Decrease Brush Size	**] / [**
Increase / Decrease Brush Softness (25%)	**Shift+] / Shift+[**
Set Tool Opacity	**Numeric Keypad 1-0**

SELECTIONS

Select All	**Ctrl+A**
Deselect / Reselect	**Ctrl+D / Ctrl+Shift+D**
Feather	**Ctrl+Alt+D**
Inverse of Selection	**Ctrl+Shift+I**

ADJUSTMENTS

Open Levels palette	**Ctrl+L**
Auto Levels	**Ctrl+Shift+L**
Open Curves *(PS only)*	**Ctrl+M**
Open Hue/Saturation palette	**Ctrl+U**
Open Color Balance palette *(PS only)*	**Ctrl+B**
Desaturate	**Ctrl+Shift+U**
Invert colours	**Ctrl+I**

CHAPTER 1
BASIC SKILLS

CROPPING, LEVELS AND CLONING – LEARN THEM RIGHT HERE!

Remember, when you see this icon, there's a video lesson of the technique on the cover DVD.

P14 CREATIVE CROPPING

Change the size and shape of your pictures to get the best out of them, and find out how you can crop to exact sizes, too.

P18 USING LEVELS

Discover how you can control your contrast using this essential imaging command, and find out what happens to your pixels in a Histogram!

LEARN WITH US

IMPROVE IMAGES BY CROPPING THEM EFFECTIVELY, CONTROLLING THEIR CONTRAST, REMOVING BLEMISHES & DISTRACTIONS, & SHARPENING THE RESULTS

P26 HEALING & PATCHING

Learn how to use the *Healing Brush* and *Spot Healing Brush* tools to remove blemishes and get perfect results every time.

P30 SHARPENING YOUR PICTURES

Almost all images need a little bit of sharpening, so we show you the right way to do it using *Unsharp Mask*.

P22 CLEANING UP YOUR PICS

Find out how to use the *Clone Stamp tool* so you can get rid of distractions in your pics and get a cleaner composition.

THERE ARE FOUR MAIN processes that every digital image has to go through between leaving the camera and being sent to a printer, and in this bonus magazine, we cover the whole lot!

Once a picture's been taken, you'll probably have some idea of what you're going to do with it. It may be destined for an online photo lab to emerge as a 6x4in print, it may be heading for a sheet of glossy A4 after a brief journey through your inkjet printer, or it may end up proudly displayed on your website for others to see and enjoy.

Workflow

Whatever the purpose of your image, it needs to fit into your imaging workflow, and this will involve it being cropped to size, and it being checked and adjusted to ensure it has a full range of tones. Once these two stages are out of the way, you'll need to scrutinise the image and clean up any blemishes or imperfections, and as a final touch, you'll need to add a little sharpening to the right areas to ensure it has the level of clarity and definition to show it off at its very best.

These four essential stages are all covered in detail, so turn the page and start developing your perfect imaging workflow...

VIDEO LESSON ON THE COVER DISC!

Ps Pse

When you see this CD-ROM logo, it means there's an in-depth video lesson on our cover disc that accompanies the technique. Watch and learn as one of our experts takes you through the project, step by step!

OPTION 1 VERTICAL 3:2 CROP

OPTION 2 PANORAMIC CROP

OPTION 3 SQUARE CROP

THE START IMAGE

FILENAME BOATS.JPG There's nothing wrong with the original composition, but with the *Crop tool* we can explore several creative treatments and come up with vertical, square and even panoramic options.

DON'T WASTE TIME RETOUCHING OR ADJUSTING AREAS THAT MAY END UP BEING CROPPED OUT

CREATIVE CROPPING

STRENGTHEN YOUR COMPOSITIONS OR MAKE SPECIFIC-SIZED IMAGES USING THE CROP TOOL

VIDEO LESSON ON THE COVER DISC!

Ps Pse

AFTER YOU'VE TRANSFERRED your pictures onto your PC and decided which ones you're going to keep, the first job in the creative workflow is cropping. The reason for this is you don't want to start retouching or adjusting the complete image, because that may involve spending time and effort on areas that could end up being cropped out. To select the *Crop tool*, click on the icon in the Toolbox or hit *C* on the keyboard. It may be covered by the *Recompose tool* if you're using Elements, so if this is the case, just hit *C* again to bring it up. Once the tool is active, check in the Options bar at the top of the screen and you'll see the *Aspect Ratio, Width, Height* and *Resolution* boxes.

Cropping options

These boxes have everything you need for nicely controlled crops, and if you click the downward facing arrow on the first box, you'll see a selection of different sized crop presets in the list.

No restriction gives you the freedom to crop however you want simply by dragging the mouse over the screen to form a marquee, and *Use Photo Ratio* (*Front Image* in Photoshop) means your cropped image will have the same dimensions as your original pic. To adjust the crop, just pull in any of the six handles, and if you want to keep your crop square, hold down the *Shift* key with *No Restriction* selected in the Options bar. The other presets are self explanatory.

Once you've drawn out your crop, you can rotate it by dragging the mouse outside the marquee, and when you're happy, you can either click the green tick, double-click inside the marquee or hit *Return* on the keyboard.

TURN THE PAGE FOR MORE ADVICE

GOING FOR SPECIFIC OR CUSTOM-SIZED CROPS

There are many times when photographers will need to crop their images to a specific size, such as when you're sending prints off to a lab or changing the size of an image to match a particular paper size, framing option or design layout.

In this example, we'll assume you want to make an A4-sized print from your inkjet printer, but the principle and methods are the same whether you're making a 6x4in print to upload to an online lab or a big panoramic picture to go in a special frame you've bought.

> IT'S EASY TO MAKE CUSTOM-SIZED CROPS, WHETHER IT'S FOR A LAB OR HOME INKJET

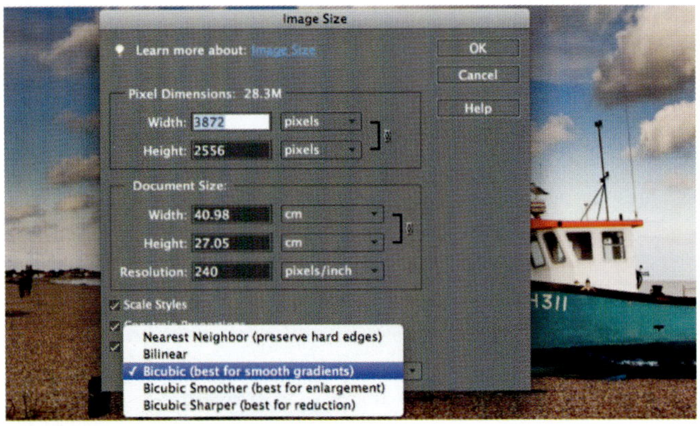

1 **START SET INTERPOLATION TYPE.** This is the stage that everybody forgets, but it's important to check how your images will be resized when you crop them. Go to *Image→Resize→ Image Size* (*Image→Image Size* in Photoshop) and set the interpolation type to the most appropriate. For most uses this will be *Bicubic*, though for graphical images like pop art, *Nearest Neighbour* will work better.

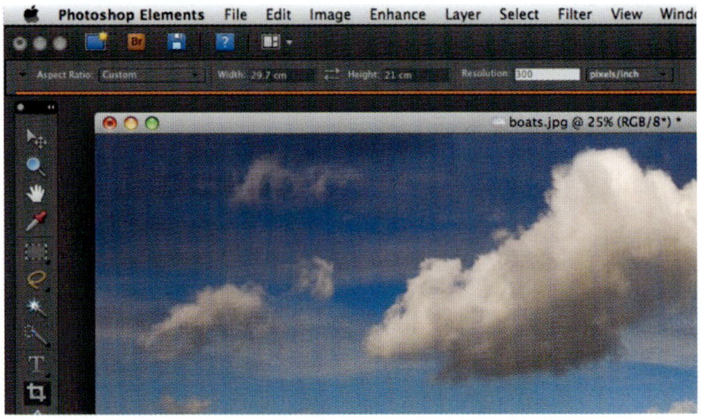

2 **SET THE DIMENSIONS.** Open the image and select the *Crop tool* from the toolbox. In the Options bar, type in the dimensions you want. For a full A4 print, we went for the measurements of *29.7cm Width*, *21cm Height*, and we set the *Resolution* to *300 pixels per inch*. This setting will give cracking quality for prints, but if your crop is for web use, you'll only need *72 pixels per inch*.

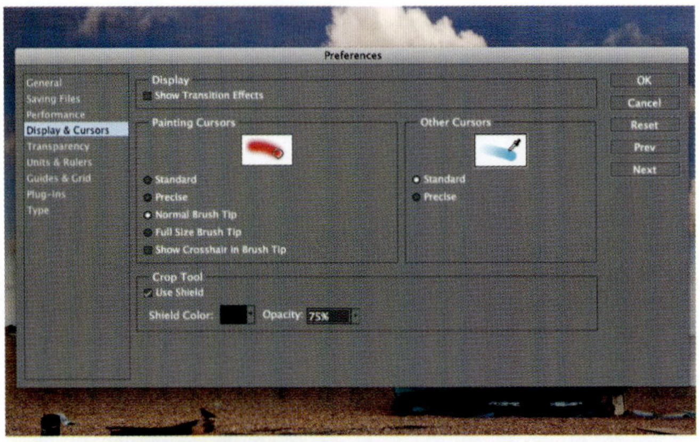

3 **MAKE THE CROP.** Your aspect ratio will be restricted to the dimensions you've put in, so drag out a marquee over the image, and get the best composition. The Shield (the bit you're cropping out) is black with a *75% Opacity*, but if you want to change this to a different colour or make it more or less opaque, just go to *Edit→ Preferences* and you can change it under *Displays and Cursors*.

4 **FINISH COMPLETE THE CROP.** You can rotate the crop by dragging the mouse outside the marquee (you'll see the cursor change to a double-headed arrow), and when you've got the crop you desire, hit *Enter*, click the tick, or double-click inside the bounding box to make it happen. If you change your mind and don't want to crop, just hit *Esc* or click the red cross to abandon the changes.

CROPPING WITH THE RECTANGULAR MARQUEE TOOL

A little known alternative to the *Crop tool* is the *Rectangular Marquee tool*, and here you can opt for a *Fixed Ratio* (such as 3:2, 16:9, 6:17 or whatever is most appropriate for your output use) or you can go for a *Fixed Size*, measured in *cm*, *in* or *px*. Once you've dragged out the crop you want, all you have to do is go to *Edit→Crop*, and the excess outside the *Rectangular Marquee* will be deleted. This method of cropping actually works with any Selection tool, such as the *Elliptical Marquee* or even the *Lasso tool*, but it's hard to find genuine uses for these situations, so the best bet is to stick with the *Rectangular Marquee* if the regular *Crop tool* doesn't give you the functionality you're after.

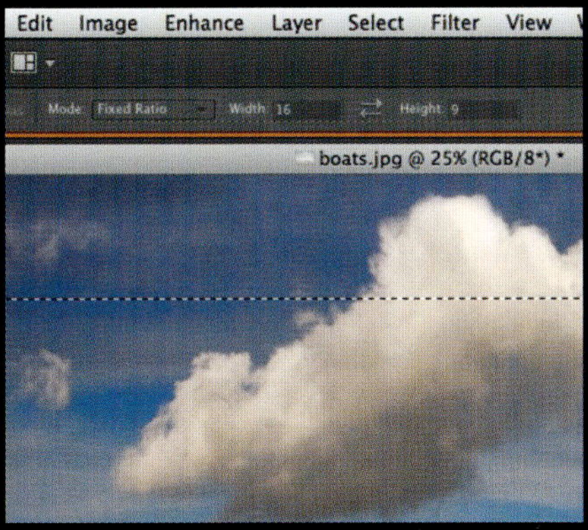

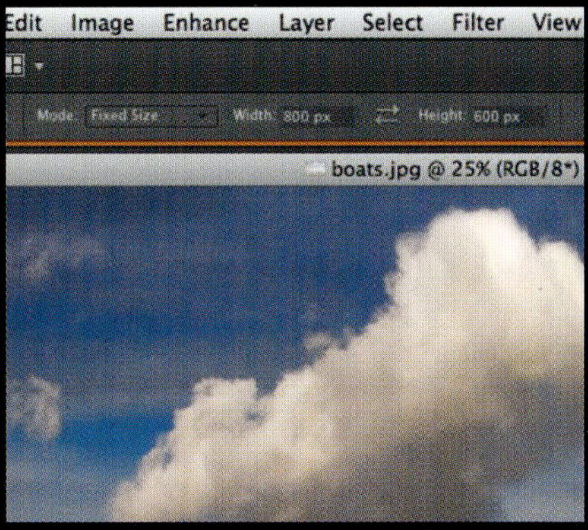

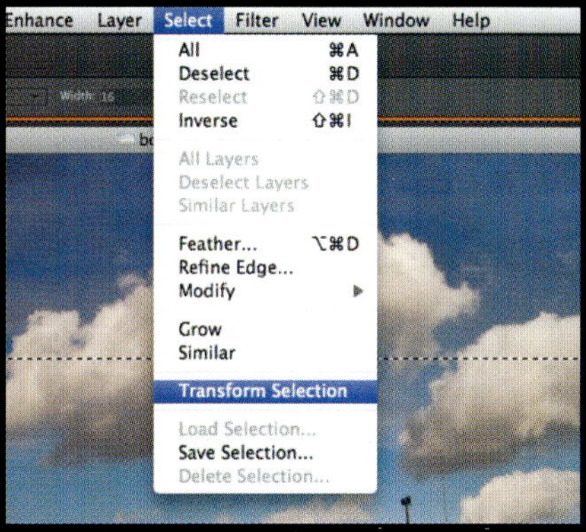

1 **FIXED RATIO CROPS.** If you want to see how an image looks at a crop ratio of 16:9, 17:6, 10:8 or anything else, then instead of setting this up in the *Crop tool*, just select the *Rectangular Marquee* and choose *Fixed Ratio* under *Mode* in the options bar. Key in the width-to-height ratio you want to try and then drag the Marquee across the image. Go to *Image→Crop* if you like it!

2 **FIXED SIZE CROPS.** There are times - particularly for web and email use - when you need to make a crop of a specific size (eg: 800x600px). To do this, select the *Rectangular Marquee*, and then pick *Fixed Size* under *Mode* in the Options bar. Enter your dimensions, and when you click on the pic, you'll see the marquee appear at that size. Go to *Image→Crop* and the job's done.

3 **TRANSFORMING SELECTIONS.** If you want to change the shape of your Marquee after you've dragged it out, you can't just hit *Ctrl+T* and start pulling the handles as you'll distort the pic. Instead, go to *Select→Transform Selection*, and you can then reshape it to your heart's content without affecting the image. When you're happy, hit *Enter* to confirm the new shape.

KNOWLEDGE DIFFERENCES IN PHOTOSHOP'S CROP TOOL

There are a few tweaks in the functionality of the *Crop tool* between Elements and the full version, so to ensure users of Photoshop are up to speed, here are the major differences.

- **In Photoshop, *C* on the keyboard will cycle through the *Crop tool* and the *Slice tools* (there's no *Recompose tool* to worry about).**
- **The *Shield* and its *Opacity* can be changed directly in the Options bar, so you don't have to go into *Preferences*.**
- **The third difference is a subtle one, but it can be useful when trying out dynamic cropping treatments. When you rotate a crop, you'll notice that it revolves around a small target icon at the centre of the crop's marquee. In Elements this point is fixed, but in Photoshop it's floating, so you can move it anywhere inside (or outside) the bounding box. With portraits, place this between the subject's eyes to assess different angles without having to reposition the crop.**

GET STARTED WITH LEVELS

Ps Pse

LEVELS IS AN IMPORTANT TOOL FOR ASSESSING AND SORTING OUT CONTRAST. WE EXPLAIN WHAT IT DOES AND HOW TO USE IT

A DIGITAL IMAGE CONSISTS of millions of tiny squares called picture elements or pixels. Up close, these squares each have a particular brightness and solid colour, but provided you have enough of them making up an image, the squareness appears to 'round off' and forms continuous shapes and smooth, graduated shades of colour.

What can be useful to the photographer is to know how well distributed the darker and brighter pixels are in a scene, and the graph displayed by the *Levels palette* shows exactly this. Dark and bright tones are important because they determine the tonal range of the image, and in turn, this controls the contrast. Having an objective graph to show the different tones is handy, as it reveals whether you have true black and true white in the image - and hence a full range of tones - or whether you have an image lacking in contrast that only stretches from dark grey to light grey.

Histograms

The graph representing all this is called a Histogram and gives a view of the distribution of all the pixels in the image. Black pixels are positioned on the left edge of the graph, white pixels are placed over on the right, and all the other shades are shown in-between according to how dark or how bright they are. The pixels sharing the same brightness values are stacked on top of each other in a Histogram, so if you had an image that was half-black and half-white, you'd simply have a vertical line on the left of the graph to show the big pile of black pixels, and a vertical line on the right to show the stack of white pixels. The two lines would be the same height if the image was exactly half and half, but if the black occupied less of the area compared to the white, then the black line would be lower than the white one, as fewer black pixels would be present overall.

So far so good, but to make sure we're crystal clear about Histograms, it's important to understand that how the pixels are arranged in the image itself has no bearing on the matter - only the brightness of the pixels is shown. Therefore, if we decided to create a checkerboard picture with exactly the same number of white and black squares in the image, the Histogram would look *exactly* the same as our half-white, half-black picture. All we're seeing is the *number* of dark and light pixels and how dark or bright they are. Without the image itself to look at, we have no clues as to how the pixels themselves are actually arranged.

The Levels palette

The *Levels palette* gives a Histogram display and reveals all this important information, but what's amazing is that it's adjustable, too. That means if you don't have any true black or true white, then you can adjust the sliders under the graph and turn light grey into white and dark grey into black. This gives your image the full range of tones you're after, and if you want to go further, you can also adjust the mid-point to lighten or darken the midtones of the pic. Just slide it a little to the left or right to accomplish this.

THE LEVELS PALETTE GIVES A HISTOGRAM DISPLAY, BUT IT'S ADJUSTABLE, TOO

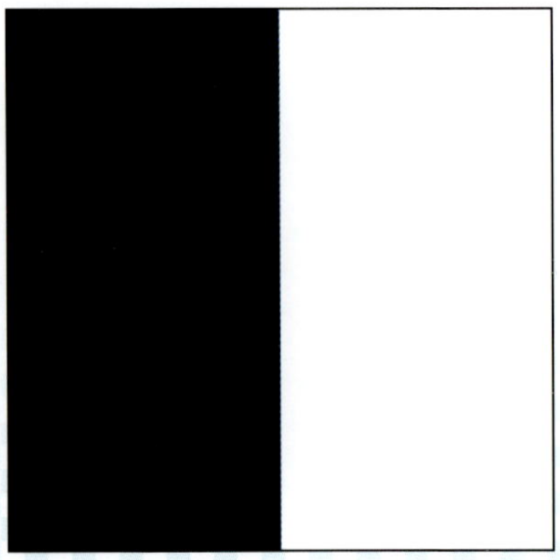

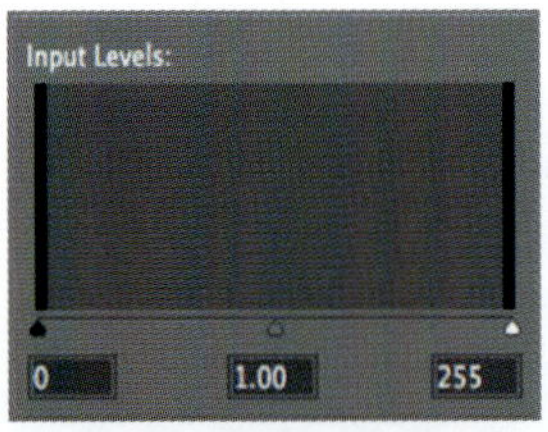

This half & half pic gives a Histogram with a stack of black pixels (the '0' line on the left) and an equal number of white pixels (the '255' line on the right).

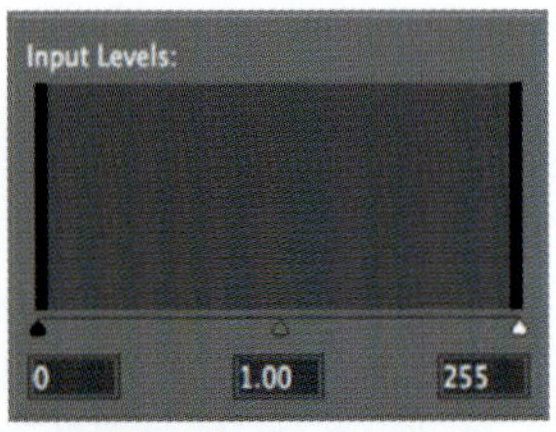

Here, the pic has changed, but the Histogram is the same because we have the same number of black and white pixels - even though they're arranged differently.

TOP TIP
Always check and adjust Levels before printing, as it's all too easy to waste paper and ink.

GETTING TO KNOW THE LEVELS PALETTE

CHANNEL BOX

Leave this on *RGB* to make contrast adjustments, or select the individual *Red*, *Green* and *Blue* Channels to adjust the colour balance of the pic.

HISTOGRAM

This is a graph with all the pixels of the same tonal values stacked on top of each other. Gaps at either end (as seen here) reveal the lack of true black or white pixels in the image.

INPUT LEVELS

These three sliders (and the boxes beneath) reveal the input settings for black, mid grey and white, so you can change the black and white points of the image and alter the contrast.

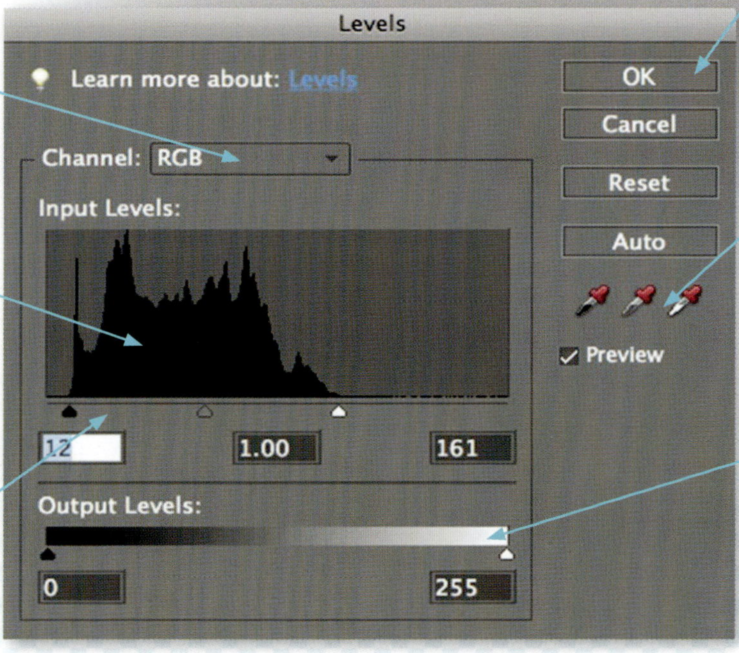

BUTTONS

OK processes the Levels adjustment you've made, *Cancel* quits out of the palette, *Reset* aborts the change and *Auto* is the software's best guess. Avoid the last one, as it's seldom any use!

EYEDROPPERS

These handy tools let you select black, white and midtone values by clicking directly on the image. Handy for assessing contrast and colour balance changes really quickly.

OUTPUT LEVELS

These are the Black and White settings for your final image, so leave them on *0* for true black and *255* for true white unless you have a good reason to do otherwise!

TURN OVER & SEE LEVELS IN ACTION

LEVELS IN ACTION

The easiest way to learn about the power of *Levels* is to use them for real! On the disc you'll find an image called *VENICE.jpg*, and it's in a sorry state. The picture is under-exposed for starters, meaning there's no true white in the image, and to make it worse, contrast is very low and as a result, there's no true black in the shadows, either.

Looking at it on screen, it'd be easy to simply write it off and consign it to the *Recycle Bin*, but because our problems are all to do with exposure and contrast, there's a good chance that we can rescue the shot with a *Levels* adjustment and make it quite presentable.

> THERE'S A GOOD CHANCE WE CAN RESCUE THE SHOT WITH A LEVELS ADJUSTMENT

THE START IMAGE

FILENAME
VENICE.JPG
The whole thing is under-exposed and lacking in contrast, so we need *Levels* to help us out in a big way on this one!

DULL WHITES
With no true white in the image, we need to force the brightest highlight to be pure white.

MURKY BLACKS
There are only dark greys as the deepest shadows, so with Levels we can turn these to true black.

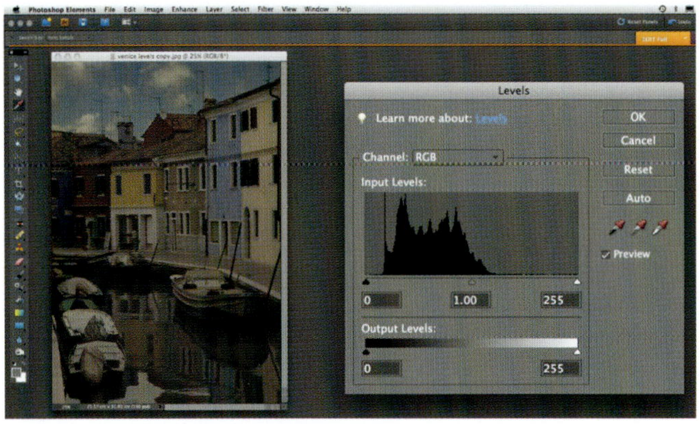

1 **START** **CHECK THE HISTOGRAM.** Open up *VENICE.jpg* from the disc, and then open the *Levels palette* with the shortcut *Ctrl+L*. Look at the Histogram and you'll see that there are 'gaps' at both ends of the graph. This means that there's no true black or true white present, and that's why the whole image looks grey and murky and is lacking in contrast.

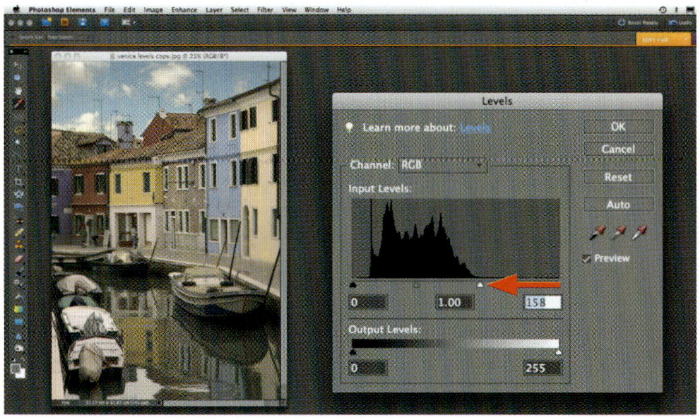

2 **SORT OUT YOUR WHITES.** Click on the white point slider at the right-hand side of the graph and move it inwards until it meets the graph itself. You'll see the pic get brighter, and that's because we're forcing the light grey pixels to be white. The more you move it inwards, the more grey tones will become white, so leave it just on the edge (a setting of around *158* on this example) to avoid burn-out.

3 **FIX THE SHADOWS.** At the other end of the scale, grab the Black point slider and move it to the right to meet the graph. Here, you're making the dark grey pixels become black, so are increasing contrast at the opposite end of the tonal range. You'll notice that the image starts to look bad if you go too far, so leave the slider on the left-hand edge of the Histogram (a setting of around *21* with this pic).

4 **FINISH** **ADJUST THE MIDTONES.** Now you've set your black & white points, you have a full range of tones, so all that's left is to adjust the midtones. The default value for the midtones is 1.0, so you can always revert back, but move the slider to the left and right and you'll see how it changes the overall brightness without affecting the black and white points you've set. Click *OK*.

THE FINAL IMAGE
After a *Levels* tweak, the murky shadows and dull, grey highlights are gone, giving this classic Venetian scene a new lease of life.

HOW TO CLEAN UP YOUR PICS

IMPROVE YOUR IMAGES USING THE CLONE STAMP TOOL IN PHOTOSHOP OR ELEMENTS

VIDEO LESSON ON THE COVER DISC!

Ps Pse

ONE OF THE MANY things that marks working with digital images out from film is the ease in which you can repair parts of a picture, or remove distracting elements. This is of enormous benefit to you as a photographer because it lets you clean up landscape scenes or hide your subject's blemishes in a portrait - and generally improve the look and feel of your images.

This process of repair and improvement comes via several tools in Photoshop, the *Clone Stamp tool*, the *Healing brush*, the *Spot Healing brush* and, occasionally, the *Patch tool* - and it's the first of these we'll look at in this lesson. In the example image you'll see how we've used the *Clone Stamp tool* to remove some of the rocks in this scene and refine the composition.

Copying pixels

The *Clone Stamp tool* works in a similar way to the *Brush tool* in Photoshop, but instead of painting colours onto your picture, it copies or 'samples' pixels from another part of the picture - an area you've defined beforehand.

You can vary the size of the sample, its strength and how it copies the pixels, as you'll discover in this lesson. We'll start with a simple graphic to show how it works, then move on to a real image.

THE CLONE STAMP TOOL COPIES PIXELS FROM ONE PART OF YOUR PIC TO ANOTHER...

THE START IMAGE

FILENAME KESWICK.JPG This image has an ideal foreground subject in the form of the semi-submerged fallen branch, but all the rocks make it look a little too cluttered.

DISTRACTING ROCKS

The jumble of rocks in the water is detracting from the simple, striking shape of this semi-sunken branch.

TRICKY REFLECTIONS

Removing the rock that breaks up the branch's reflection will require some careful cloning so we don't disturb the line.

USING THE CLONE OVERLAY FEATURE

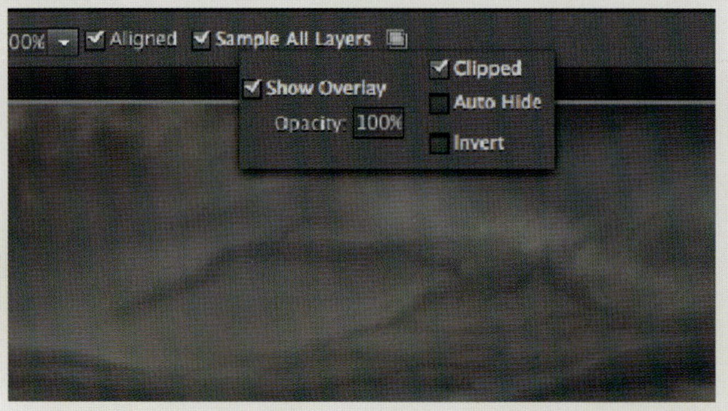

More recent versions of Photoshop and Elements include a feature called the *Clone Overlay*. This provides a preview of the pixels you're about to clone onto the image and is therefore very useful in helping you avoid copying unwanted areas. The feature may need to be turned on, though, so in Elements click on the *Show Clone Overlay Options* icon (the two overlapping squares) and make sure that *Show Overlay* is ticked. In Photoshop, again in the Options bar, click on the *Toggle Clone Source Panel* button and you'll find similar options. You'll notice that you can also vary the *Opacity* of the *Clone Overlay*, so you can still see the background onto which you'll be copying pixels. The *Clipped* option should also be ticked which will set the *Overlay* to your current brush size.

THE FINAL IMAGE

Using the *Clone Stamp tool* to remove unwanted distractions leads to a simpler and more effective composition in this landscape image.

TURN THE PAGE FOR MORE ADVICE

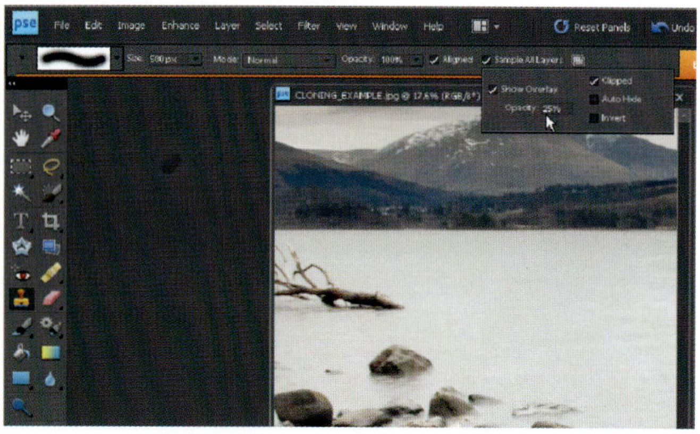

1

START SET UP THE CLONE TOOL. Open the picture called *KESWICK.jpg* from the disc and then choose the *Clone Stamp tool* from the Toolbox (keyboard shortcut, *S*). In the Options bar move along to the *Clone Overlay Options* button (the *Clone Source Panel* toggle in Photoshop), click it and make sure that the *Show Overlay* and *Clipped* options are ticked.

2

ADD A NEW LAYER. Open the *Layers palette* (*Window➔ Layers*) and then either click the *Create New Layer* or go to *Layer➔New Layer...* and click *OK*. Go back to the Options bar and make sure that the *Aligned* and *Sample All Layers* are both ticked – the latter will allow you to clone onto the new Layer (*Layer 1*), rather than the *Background* Layer, so you can correct any mistakes more easily.

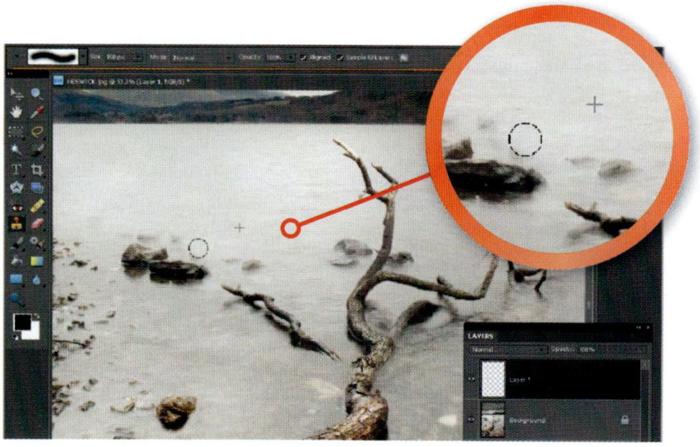

3

START CLONING. Still in the Options bar, click the *Brush Presets* drop-down and choose a *150px* soft-edged brush. Now hold the *Alt* key down to bring up the sample point picker a nd, working horizontally to the rock you want to remove, click to sample a 'clean' area of water. Release the *Alt* key to confirm the sample point, then paint over the rock.

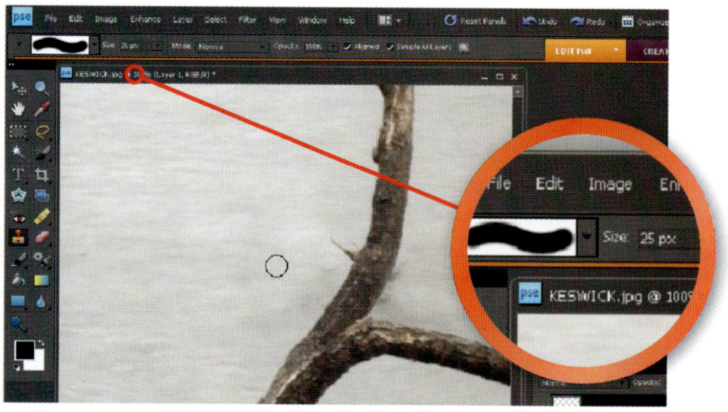

4

CHANGE THE BRUSH. When you reach a tricky area like this rock which is sat behind a branch, you'll need to harden the edge of the *Clone Stamp tool*. To do this, hold *Shift* and press the *]* key a few times. Now you can clone up to the edge of the branch as before. To soften any hard edges left over, press *Shift+[* to soften the edge and work over the area again.

5

REBUILDING WORK. Another tricky part of this image is at the bottom, where a rock we want to remove runs across the reflection of the branch. Here, we'll need to rebuild the reflection, following its shape. The *Clone Overlay* really helps here, so *Alt-click* on the edge of the reflection to sample it and use the preview to line up where you paint.

6

CHECK YOUR WORK. In the *Layers palette*, click the *Layer visibility icon* (the eye symbol) next to *Layer 1* on and off to check your cloning work. If you want to correct anything, use the *Eraser tool* (set to *100% Opacity*) and, making sure that *Layer 1* is highlighted in the *Layers palette*, click on the part of the image that you want to delete.

7 **FLATTEN THE IMAGE.** When you're happy with the cloning work that you've done and you don't want to make any more changes, it's time to flatten your image, ready for saving or printing. Go to *Layer➔Flatten Image* or press *Ctrl+E* on the keyboard and you'll go back to a single *Background* Layer.

8 FINISH **SAVE YOUR WORK.** The final thing to do is record the changes you've made to the picture, but instead of saving over the original, it's sensible to save a copy of the pic, just in case you want to return to the uncloned version later. To do this, go to *File➔Save As...*, pick *JPEG* and give it a new file name. Click *OK*, then set the *Quality* to *10* or *12*.

EXPERT ADVICE TIPS FOR GOOD CLONING

It's easy to get up and running with the *Clone Stamp tool*, but there are a few golden rules to observe if you want the best results. Follow them and you'll be able to make perfect, photo realistic alterations to your digital images...

TIP 1 Avoid repeating patterns

When you copy pixels from one part of an image to another, it's easy to create a repeating pattern, which will look unnatural and be a dead giveaway that you've made adjustments in that area. To prevent this, make sure the *Aligned* option is ticked and keep a close eye on the areas you've cloned, using a smaller brush to copy over any parts that look out of the ordinary.

TIP 2 Follow the lines

If you're cloning along a hard edge or a line in an image – like the branch's reflection in our example – make sure you keep it consistent and don't change its course from the original. Use the *Clone Overlay* preview as a guide or make a Selection along the edge first using one of the Lasso tools.

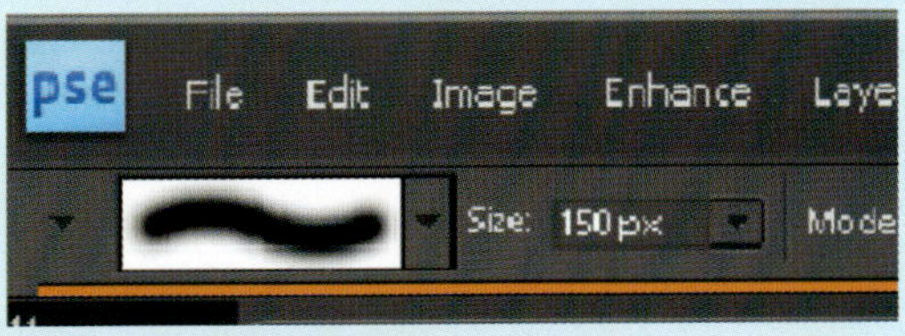

TIP 3 Vary the softness

Cloning on different areas of your image requires varying the levels of brush hardness – cloning water or sky is best done with a soft-edged brush, while complex textures like grass or concrete work better with harder brushes, minimising the amount of ghosting. Use *Shift+[* and *Shift+]* to vary hardness.

HEALING & PATCHING

LEARN HOW TO REMOVE BLEMISHES WITH THE HEALING BRUSH TOOL

THE HEALING BRUSH is an essential tool for all digital photographers. With it you can quickly and easily correct a variety of imperfections on all manner of subjects to help clean up images and improve their quality.

It works in a similar way to the *Clone Stamp tool* by copying or sampling pixels chosen by you, and letting you brush them onto another area of the picture. Unlike the *Clone Stamp tool*, however, the *Healing Brush* also attempts to blend shades and textures in the process, allowing for more seamless corrections. Although the *Healing Brush* is extremely versatile and can be used in a variety of different ways, it's most commonly used on portraits for removing blemishes and skin defects.

Sample point

When healing, it's worth noting that as you move the cursor, the sample point - marked as a cross - will mirror your cursor's movement. Therefore, be careful when healing in smaller areas as the moving sample point may run over unwanted details and copy them to the area you're correcting.

THE START IMAGE

FILENAME LORRAINE.JPG Our start image, which is available on the disc, exhibits some common editing challenges - an ideal job for the *Healing Brush tool*.

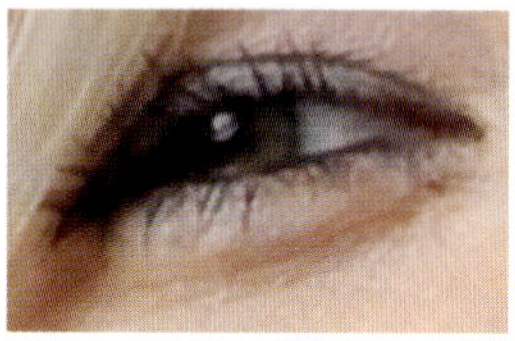

SMILE LINES

Creases in the skin - usually around the eyes and mouth - are often seen as undesirable and can easily be removed.

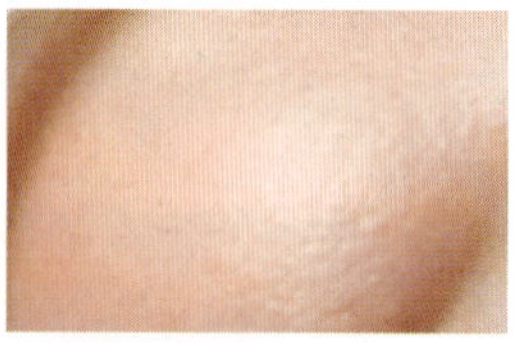

SHINY SKIN

When bright light is cast onto a subject, it can sometimes cause skin to appear shiny - this can be corrected, too.

BLEMISHES

No area of skin is completely devoid of any 'flaws', and blemishes of some sort are inevitable. With the *Healing Brush tool* however, imperfections can be quickly dispatched with just a few simple clicks.

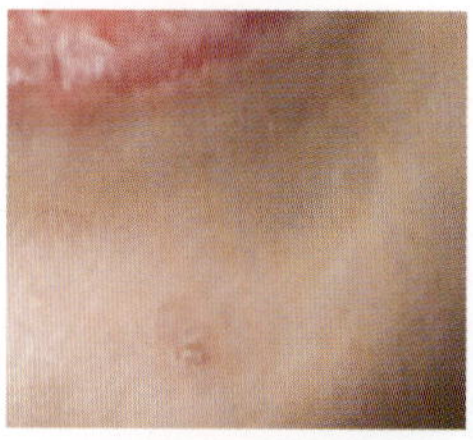

THE FINAL IMAGE

Removing blemishes and achieving flawless skin is simple with the help of the *Healing Brush tool.*

VIDEO LESSON ON THE COVER DISC!

Ps Pse

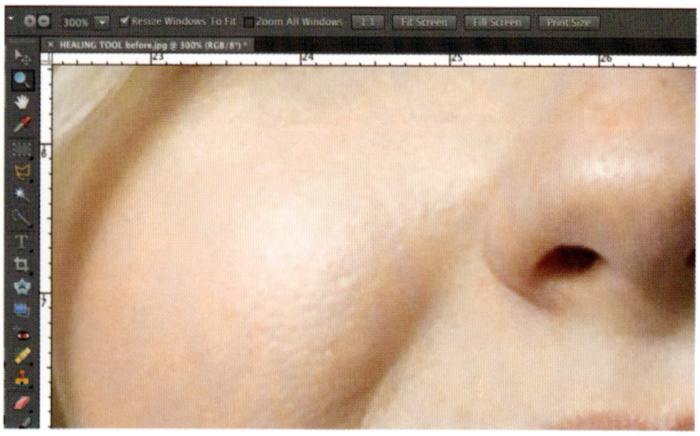

1 **START BRUSH SIZE.** Pick the *Healing Brush tool* from the Toolbox, click the *Brush picker* and set *Size* to around *25px* and *Hardness* to *0%*. Also, check that *Sample* is picked, rather than *Pattern*. It's best to use a soft brush when working on large areas, as this ensures that any healing will blend smoothly into the original – healing with a hard-edged brush can leave a more noticeable outline.

2 **GET IN CLOSE.** When healing, it helps to try to get in close to the area you're working on. Do this by either selecting the *Zoom tool (Z)* from the Toolbox and left-clicking on the section of your image you wish to magnify, or by pressing *Ctrl++*. This will ensure that any brush strokes you make are accurate, so you can check that the healing process has worked correctly.

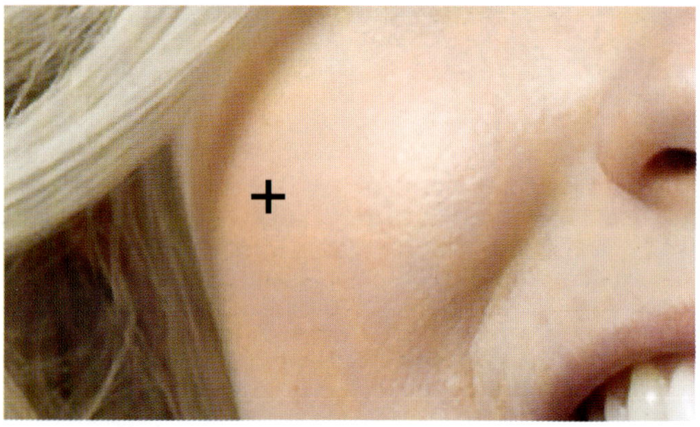

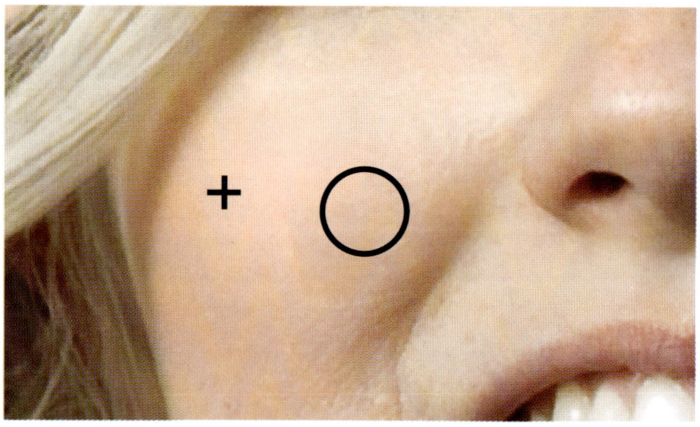

3 **SET THE SAMPLE POINT.** Locate the area that you want to repair. Then, while holding down the *Alt* key, left-click in an area that's nearby – somewhere which is clear and unmarked and of a similar tone. This will set a sample point (marked by a cross) which Photoshop or Elements will then take information from in order to heal the affected area.

4 **START TO HEAL.** With a sample point successfully set, carefully brush over the area you want to heal. Try to use smooth, continuous brush strokes, rather than clicking repeatedly, to create an even finish. Healing can be hit or miss at times so, if you feel like you need to have another go at a brush stroke, simply press *Ctrl+Z* to undo a step.

KNOWLEDGE THE PATCH TOOL IN PHOTOSHOP

Anyone with a full version of Photoshop may notice the *Patch tool* within their Toolbox. The *Patch tool* is used to quickly heal large areas of an image in a single Selection – here's how it works...

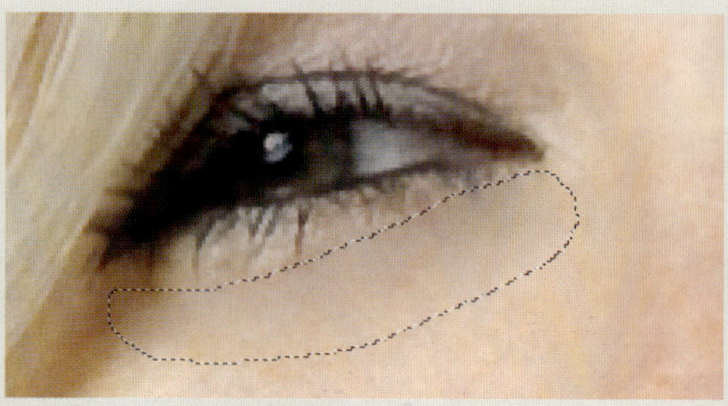

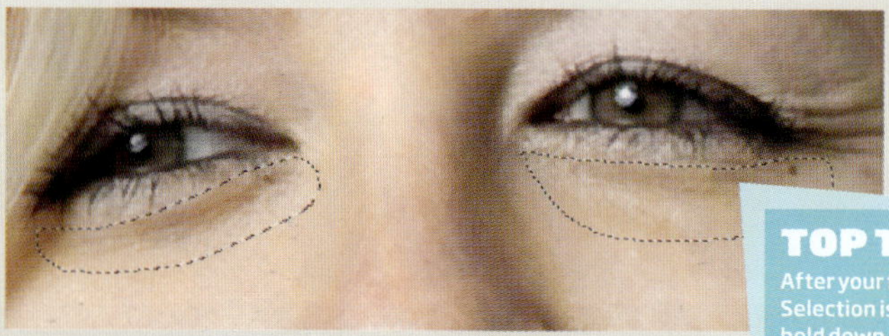

- **Grab the *Patch tool* from the Toolbox and with it set to *Source* in the Options bar, mark out an area of your image that you'd like to heal by drawing around it.**
- **With the Selection made, move your cursor into the centre of the 'marching ants', and then drag it to another section of the image that you want to use as a sample point.**
- **Release the left mouse button to merge the two areas together and successfully perform the healing process.**

TOP TIP
After your first Selection is made, hold down *Shift* to include further areas of your pic in the Selection.

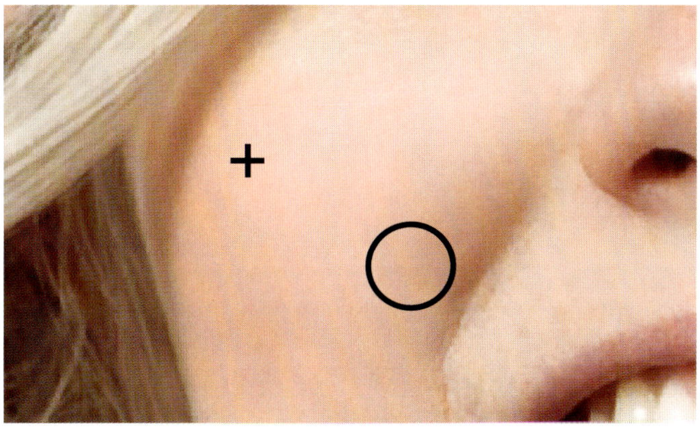

5 **REPEAT.** When trying to heal large areas in an image, it'll often be impossible to tackle the whole thing in one go. Therefore, take your time, and make smaller but more accurate brush strokes. If you need to reset your sample point, simply hold down the *Alt* key and left-click in a new location, then continue brushing.

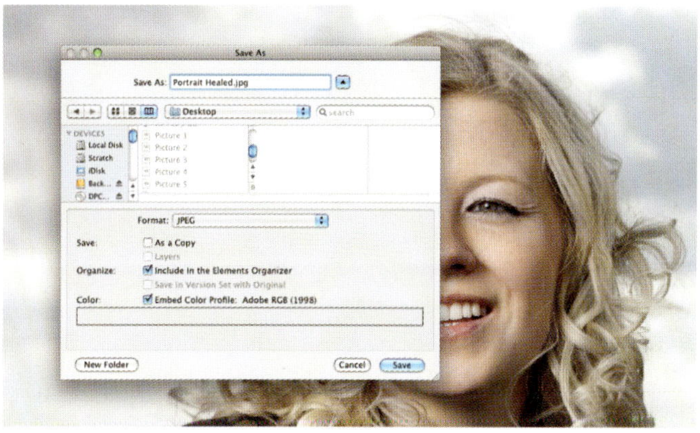

6 FINISH **SAVE YOUR WORK.** Once you're happy that all areas of the portrait have been seen to, save your work as a new file by going to *File→Save As...* Healing creates a permanent alteration to your work and once saved, you can't revert to the original, so saving your healed image as a second file lets you keep the original intact in case you ever need to revisit it.

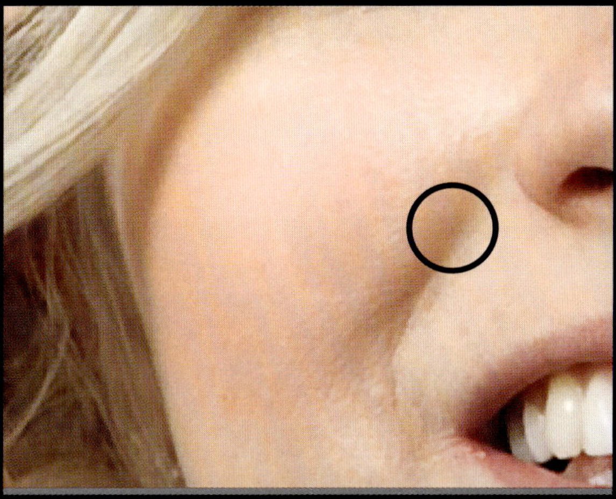

WORK FASTER WITH THE SPOT HEALING BRUSH

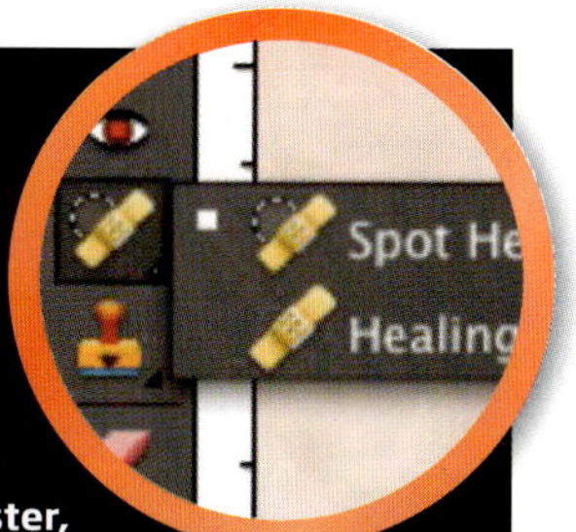

Although the *Healing Brush tool* is a fantastic way of cleaning up larger areas, if you want to work faster, the *Spot Healing Brush* can provide quick repairs when working on small areas. To find it, right-click in the Toolbox or keep pressing *J* until it appears. Working in a similar manner to its older brother, the main difference with the *Spot Healing Brush tool* is that it automatically locates a sample point from nearby pixels - rather than the user having to set one manually. For best results, in the Options bar set it to *Proximity Match* or *Content-Aware* rather than *Create Texture*. Though it's a faster option, it can occasionally struggle when working in areas of contrasting texture & colour, so keep checking your results.

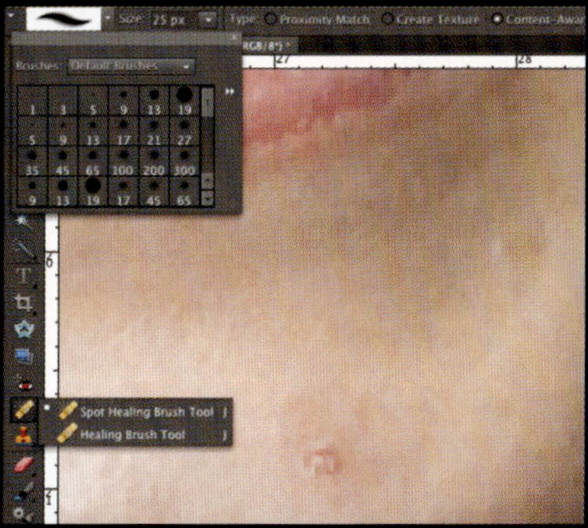

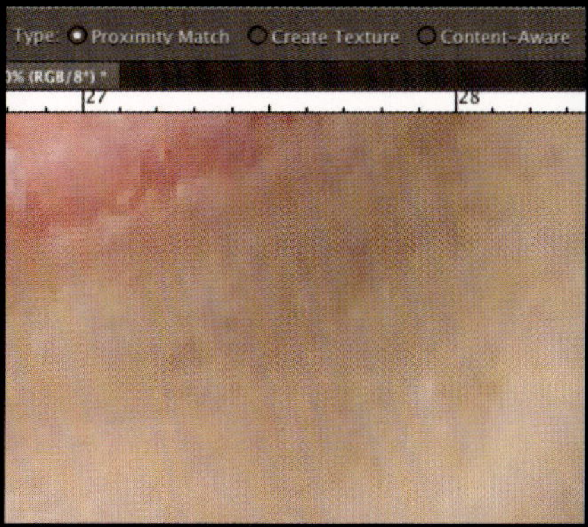

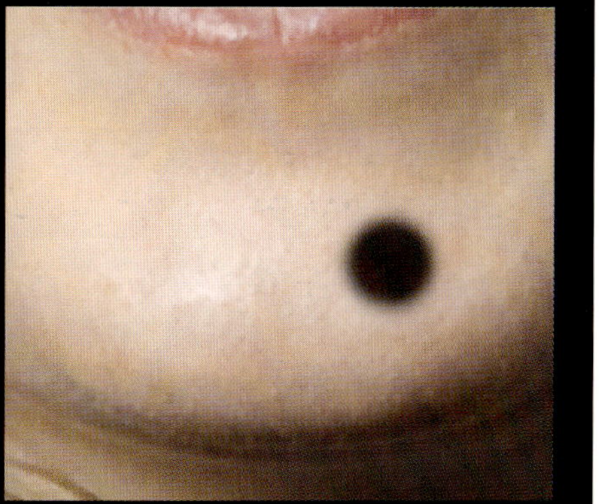

1 **SPOT HEALING TOOL.** Select the *Healing Brush tool* in the toolbox and right-click it to activate a drop-down menu. Within this menu you should see the *Spot Healing Brush tool* which can be selected by left-clicking on the icon. Once selected, make sure you choose a soft brush from the brush picker, and change the *Brush Size* to around 25px.

2 **BRUSH SETTINGS.** If you've got the latest version of Photoshop or Elements, you may notice three settings at the top of the screen - Proximity Match, Create Texture and Content Aware - make sure *Proximity Match* is selected. If you've got an older version of the software and these options aren't present, Proximity Match will already be set as default.

3 **HEALING.** Move to the area you want to repair and zoom in using the *Zoom tool (Z)*. Now, holding down the left mouse button, start to paint over and highlight the blemished area then release the mouse button once you're done. Photoshop will automatically perform the healing process. When you're finished, don't forget to save your work by going to *File→Save As*.

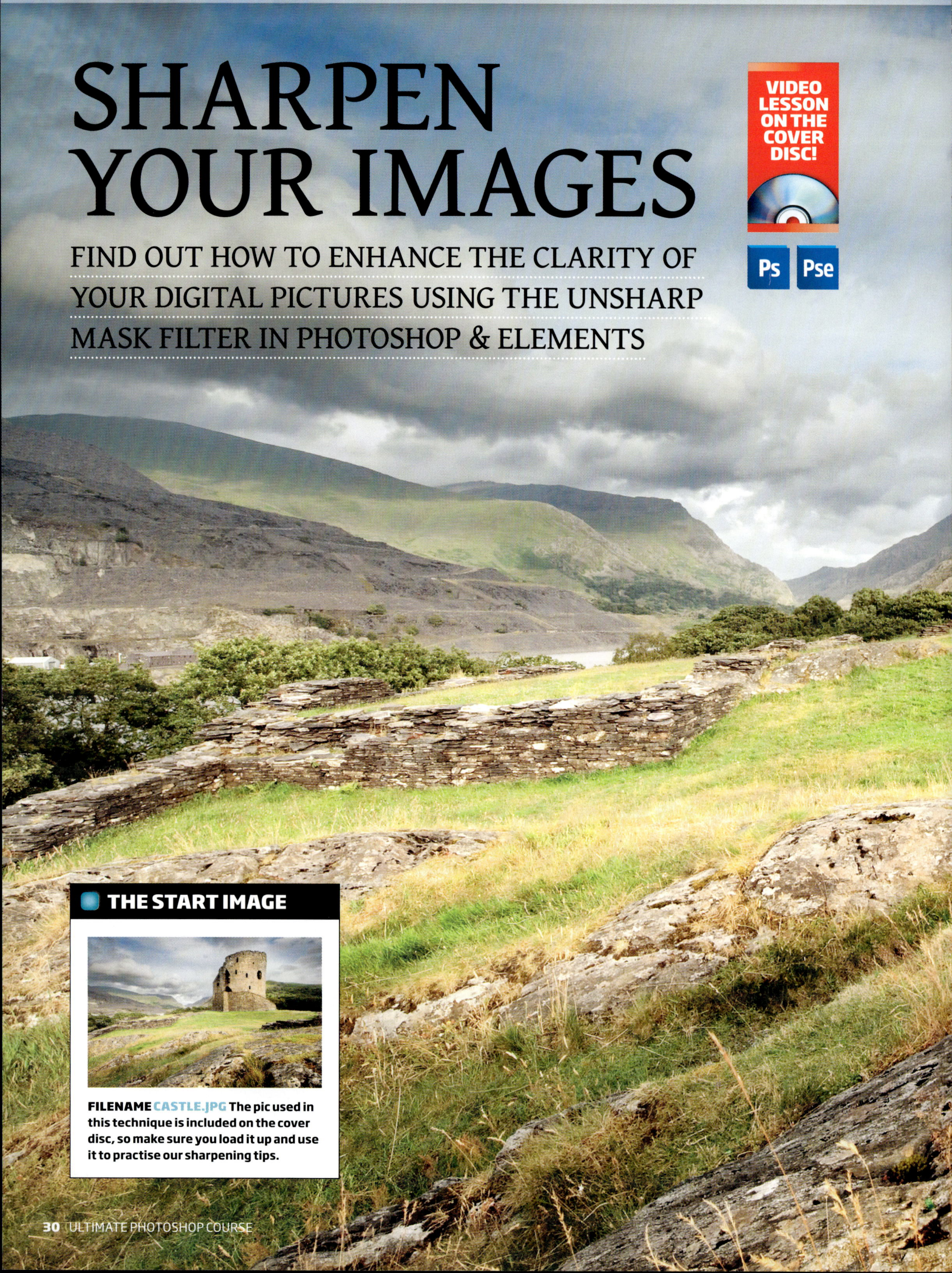

SHARPEN YOUR IMAGES

FIND OUT HOW TO ENHANCE THE CLARITY OF YOUR DIGITAL PICTURES USING THE UNSHARP MASK FILTER IN PHOTOSHOP & ELEMENTS

VIDEO LESSON ON THE COVER DISC!

Ps Pse

THE START IMAGE

FILENAME CASTLE.JPG The pic used in this technique is included on the cover disc, so make sure you load it up and use it to practise our sharpening tips.

THE FINAL IMAGE

With the right level of sharpness applied to this picture the quality of the stonework becomes much easier to make out, as does the texture in the foreground.

Applying the *Unsharp Mask* filter to your pictures can really improve the level of detail within them. Just make sure you don't overdo it or you'll create heavy fringeing that will spoil your image.

SHARPENING IS AN especially important part of digital photography and naturally comes at the end of your imaging workflow. It's necessary for a number of reasons, mainly because most images that come off your digital camera will benefit from at least a little extra clarity. This may be down to slight mis-focusing at the time of shooting, the movement of the camera at slower shutter speeds, subtle defects in your lens, or if you've shot in RAW image mode where no in-camera sharpening is applied.

Fortunately though, Photoshop or Elements allow you to add sharpness long after the event and you can also choose how and where it's applied to your pictures, too.

Unsharp Mask

In this lesson you'll learn all about sharpening in Photoshop and Elements using the *Unsharp Mask filter* and will soon be able to improve the clarity of your own pictures. First, we'll look at how the sharpening effect is applied using a simple graphic and then use those tips to improve a real photo.

It's important to realise however that using the *Unsharp Mask filter* doesn't actually change the true focus of the image, it simply increases the perception of sharpness by adding contrast along the 'edges' in a picture.

But so long as a picture isn't completely blurred you can certainly improve on what you've got, with the details in your image becoming crisper, clearer and easier to discern.

To illustrate exactly how sharpening is applied to your digital images, we've included two pictures on the cover disc. Load them into Photoshop or Elements and follow the step-by-step guide below - you'll soon understand how different settings within the *Unsharp Mask filter* will affect your pictures, how to avoid pushing the effect too far and how to make sure the sharpening effect can be applied exactly where you want it in your digital image.

FORTUNATELY PHOTOSHOP & ELEMENTS ALLOW YOU TO ADD SHARPNESS LONG AFTER SHOOTING

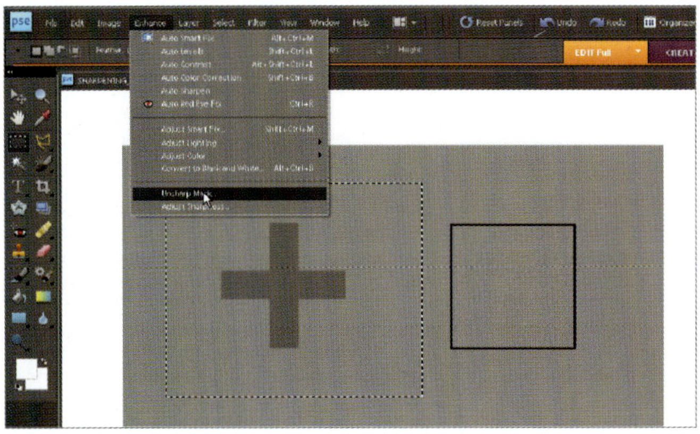

1 **START OPEN UNSHARP MASK.** Open *SHARPENING_EXAMPLE.jpg* and from the Toolbox, pick the *Rectangular Marquee tool*. Drag a Selection over the top-left cross shape, then go to *Enhance➔Unsharp Mask* (*Filter➔Sharpen➔Unsharp Mask* in Photoshop). This will launch the *Unsharp Mask* palette, with a preview pane of the sharpening in which you can click to toggle the effect.

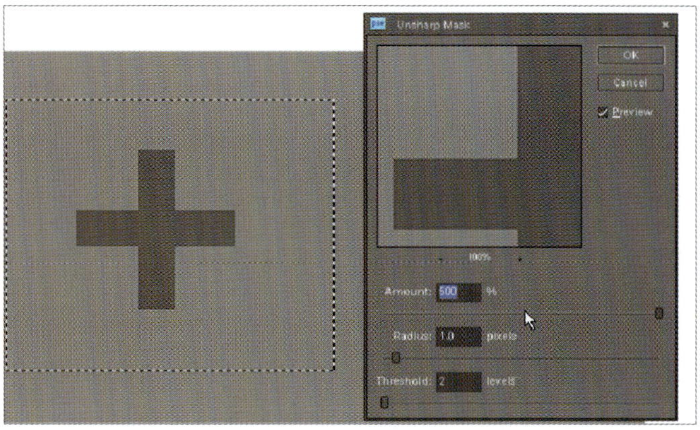

2 **ABOUT THE AMOUNT SLIDER.** The first of the sliders, the *Amount* slider, controls how much contrast is applied to the edges within your picture and therefore how pronounced and intense the sharpening effect will be. Move it to the right, to about *500%*, and you'll see one side of the cross's edge get lighter and the other darker - more contrast means more clarity.

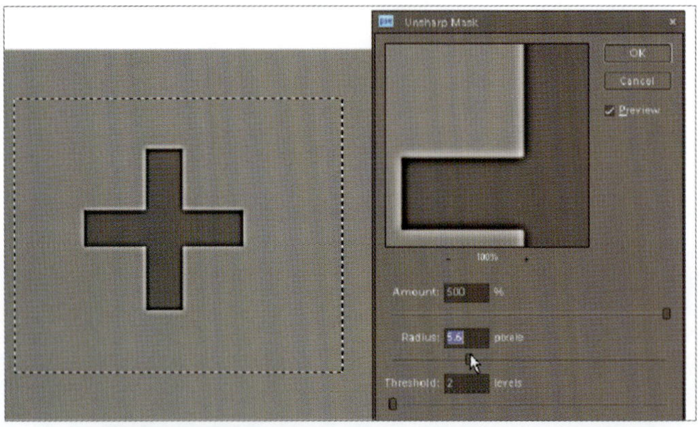

3 **ABOUT THE RADIUS SLIDER.** The second of the sliders, the *Radius* slider, controls how widely the effect of the *Amount* slider will be applied either side of an edge and is measured in pixels. Push this to the right and you'll see the darkening/lightening effect spread out from the edge of the cross. Click *OK* to apply the settings you've used.

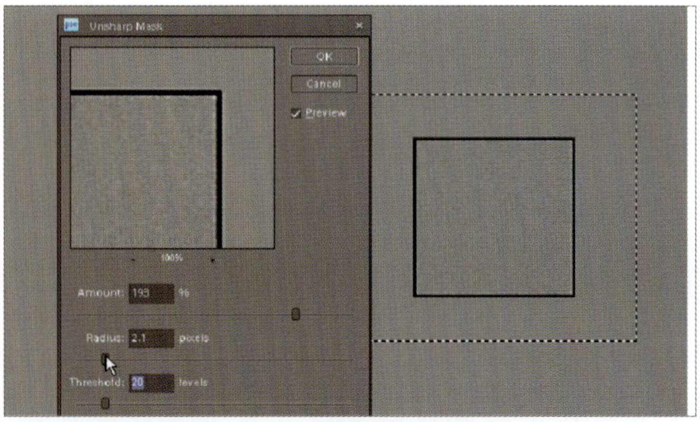

4 **ABOUT THE THRESHOLD SLIDER.** This controls what Elements thinks is an 'edge' and therefore where the sharpening effect will be applied. Select one of the squares as before and reopen the *Unsharp Mask* palette. This time move the *Threshold* slider right before you move the *Amount* and *Radius* sliders - at about *20 Levels* the line is sharpened but the Noise isn't.

EXPERT ADVICE HOW TO USE SELECTIVE SHARPENING

Even when using very small apertures, most photos feature differential focus, that is, some parts of the scene that are sharper than others. Therefore it doesn't make sense to apply sharpness globally to the entire image - you need to do it selectively. In this lesson we've copied the original image to a separate Layer, then sharpened that and deleted the parts of it we don't want to be affected by the filter. The unsharpened pixels will then show through those you've deleted. If you don't want to use Layers however, simply use the *Lasso tool* or *Polygonal Lasso tool* to select the area you want to sharpen before applying the filter - easy!

TOP TIP

Applying the sharpening to a separate layer means you can control its location easily.

5 OPEN AN IMAGE. Open *CASTLE.jpg* from the cover disc (or one of your own images, if you want). Now go to *Window→ Layers* to open the *Layers palette*, then go to *Layer→ Duplicate Layer*. You'll notice that the original image has been copied and there are now two Layers in the stack - the *Background* Layer and one called *Background Copy* onto which we'll be applying the sharpening.

6 SHARPEN THE LAYER. Now open the *Unsharp Mask filter* as in Step 1. For this image, set the *Amount* to around *150%* and the *Radius* to *0.9 pixels* and the *Theshold* to *2 Levels*. Click within the *Preview* panel to check how the sharpening is working on your images and if you're happy with the effect, click *OK* to apply the sharpening to your image.

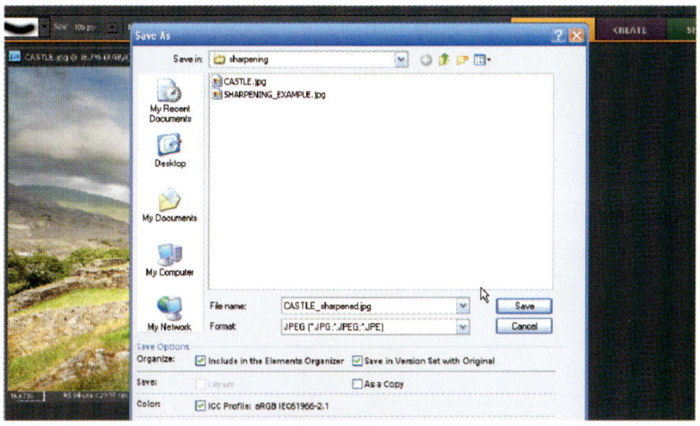

7 RESTRICT THE SHARPENING. We want to sharpen the subject and foreground, but not the sky so in the Toolbox, pick the *Eraser tool*, then set its *Size* to about *500px* and its *Opacity* to *100%*. Make sure it has a soft edge by pressing *Shift+[* a few times, then run it over the sky, deleting the sharpened pixels and letting the unsharpened ones show through from the Layer below.

8 FINISH FLATTEN & SAVE. If necessary, reduce the *Brush Size* (shortcut *[*) and run it closer to the subject. When you're done, go to *Layer→ Flatten Image*. Finally, save the sharpened version of your image as a copy by going to *File→Save As...* naming it something like *CASTLE_sharpened*, choosing *JPEG Level 10* or above. Click *OK* to save and you're all done!

CHAPTER 2
HOW TO USE LAYERS

HOW TO USE LAYERS TO IMPROVE EVERY PICTURE YOU TAKE

Remember, when you see this icon, there's a video lesson of the technique on the cover DVD.

P50 BLENDING MODES

Control how one Layer interacts with another and see how Layer Blending Modes can help you add arty effects to your pics.

LEARN WITH US!

UNDERSTANDING WHAT LAYERS ARE, HOW THEY WORK AND HOW TO USE THEM IS CRUCIAL TO THE SUCCESS OF YOUR DIGITAL IMAGING

P40 INTRODUCTION TO USING LAYERS

Layers are one of the most powerful features in Photoshop and once you get the hang of them, there's no looking back. Get started right here!

P42 LAYER MASKS MADE EASY

Hide or reveal different parts of a Layer when a Layer Mask is attached using black or white 'paint'. And if you make a mistake, you can paint it back with ease!

P54 MAKE COMPOSITES & MONTAGES USING LAYERS

Put all you've learnt in this chapter into practise and blend two photos into a convincing composite image using Layer Masks, Adjustment Layers and more.

P46 USING ADJUSTMENT LAYERS TO POP COLOUR

Make localised changes to your pictures and get all the flexibility you need using Adjustment Layers, while keeping your original image intact.

LAYERS HELP YOU EDIT YOUR PICTURES MORE EASILY & APPLY EXCITING, CREATIVE EFFECTS!

THERE ARE MANY WAYS in which software like Photoshop and Elements can help digital photographers like you make better pictures – but using Layers in your work is definitely at the top of the list.

Ever wondered how you can blend a colourful subject with a black & white background? How to apply creative textures to make arty looking pictures? Or even how to combine several different shots to make a montage or composite image? It's all down to skilful use of the Layers palette and that's something which you'll learn right here in this easy-to-follow guide.

Layers made easy

Layers work by splitting a picture into parts – parts you can then reposition, resize or recolour independently. This flexibility and freedom means you can edit your pictures much more easily and once you've learnt how to use the Layers palette you'll discover a new world of exciting and creative techniques.

To get started turn the page where you'll find a full introduction to using Layers – plus a step-by-step technique on making a basic, multi-layered image in Photoshop.

VIDEO LESSON ON THE COVER DISC!

Ps Pse

When you see this logo, it means there's an in-depth video lesson on our cover disc that accompanies the technique. Watch and learn as one of our experts takes you through the project, step by step!

HOW LAYERS MAKE UP A DIGITAL IMAGE

VIDEO LESSON ON THE COVER DISC!

Ps Pse

LET'S SEE HOW LAYERS WORK...

BLENDING MODE
This option controls how one Layer interacts with another.

LAYER OPACITY
Controls how visible the Layer is and the setting is variable from 0-100%.

PALETTE MENU
Offers quick access to many options usually found under the main Layer menu, like adding a new Layer, renaming a Layer, or duplicating a Layer.

ADJUSTMENT LAYER
An Adjustment Layer is like a digital filter, changing the appearance of all the Layers below it in the stack, but not those above it. All Adjustment Layers have Layer Masks, so you can dictate where their effects are visible.

ACTIVE LAYER
If a Layer is highlighted it's active and any painting or filter applied will only affect it and no other Layers.

LAYER VISIBILITY ICON
This eye icon can be toggled on and off to hide or reveal the Layer next to it - very useful when editing the Layers below.

LAYER THUMBNAIL
A miniature preview of the pixels on each Layer. If a chequerboard effect is visible, there are no pixels and the Layer below will show through.

LAYER MASK
Layer Masks allow you to control which parts of the corresponding Layer are visible. Any pixels covered by black will be hidden, while those covered by white are visible.

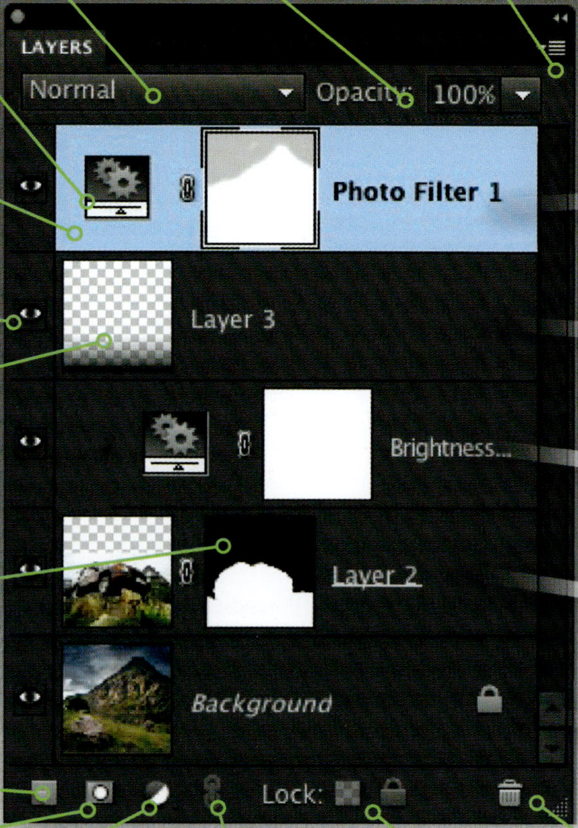

CREATE A NEW LAYER
You can click and drag a Layer onto this icon to duplicate it, or simply click it to add a new blank Layer. Holding *Alt* while clicking will allow you to rename the Layer, set its Opacity and Blending Mode.

ADD LAYER MASK
Attaches a Mask to the Layer allowing you to hide parts of it. Hold *Alt* as you click this and the Mask will be black, hiding everything on the Layer (Photoshop & Elements 9 only).

CREATE NEW FILL OR ADJUSTMENT LAYER
Click this icon and you'll get a list of the Adjustment Layers to add, such as the *Photo Filter* and *Brightness & Contrast* Adjustment Layers above.

LINK LAYERS ICON
This lets you link two or more Layers so that they can be moved around the canvas together or resized at the same time.

LOCK LAYERS
These two icons limit how a Layer can be edited.

LAYERS ARE ONE OF THE MOST POWERFUL FEATURES IN PHOTOSHOP!

IT'S ONLY WHEN you Start using Layers within Photoshop and Elements that you begin to see what it's possible to achieve with your digital pictures. Layers open the door to so many exciting creative effects that you absolutely have to learn how to use them – and once you do you'll be able to produce all sorts of different types of images. This guide is going to teach you all about Layers, what they are, how they work and how to get the best out of them.

Many photographers find using Layers off-putting and if you're new to Photoshop they can seem a tricky concept to grasp, particularly as they have no real equivalent in traditional stills photography, but we make it easy.

What are Layers?

The closest parallel to the way Layers work is in the individual cels used to make classic animated films. These would typically contain a background image on top of which was laid a transparent sheet of acetate, onto which the animator would paint. This separation meant one could be moved independently of the other, and it's exactly the same principle with Layers, except you're working with pixels instead of paint.

Take a look at the example below and you'll see how it's split into Layers – each one is a component of the final image and each adds something new to the composition. The Landrover Layer sits above the Background, its pixels covering it up in some parts while in the places where there are no pixels it lets the Background show through – just like in a cel of animation. There's another Layer to add contrast, one to darken the bottom of the pic and a final one to adjust colour.

Before we move onto subjects like this, though, we'll first look at how to use Layers in a more basic way – turn over to see how.

EACH LAYER IS A COMPONENT OF THE IMAGE AND ADDS SOMETHING TO THE WHOLE...

LAYERS REPRESENTED AS A STACK
If you could see a multi-layered image from the side, this is how it would look. All of the components sit separate from one another in the stack, like sheets of paper, but viewed from above they make up the complete image.

DELETE LAYER ICON
Either click on this to remove the active (highlighted) Layer from the image, or click and drag a Layer directly onto it from the stack to get the same effect.

TOP TIP
To see exactly how this image was made, and have a go at the technique, turn to page 54...

TURN THE PAGE FOR MORE ADVICE

HOW TO MAKE A SIMPLE LAYERED IMAGE...

AS YOU'LL SEE IN THIS GUIDE it's possible to make amazing images using the *Layers palette* in Photoshop or Elements, but if you're new to this way of working it definitely makes sense to walk before you run. Get a proper introduction to the Layers palette though and you'll be perfectly equipped to use it more creatively in your digital projects.

On these pages you'll find a simple introduction to using Layers. We'll look at some of the basic tools and techniques for using the palette, showing you how to make new Layers, copy pixels from one Layer to another, change their size and position, reorder them in the stack, change their opacity, and more.

And it's not just dull theory! Follow the steps and you'll not only learn how Layers work, but also create a pleasing frame for your photos. So load up your copy of Photoshop or Elements and get cracking!

Follow this simple tutorial and you'll find out how the Layers palette works. Plus you'll get to make a handy frame for your images, so it's a great way to learn.

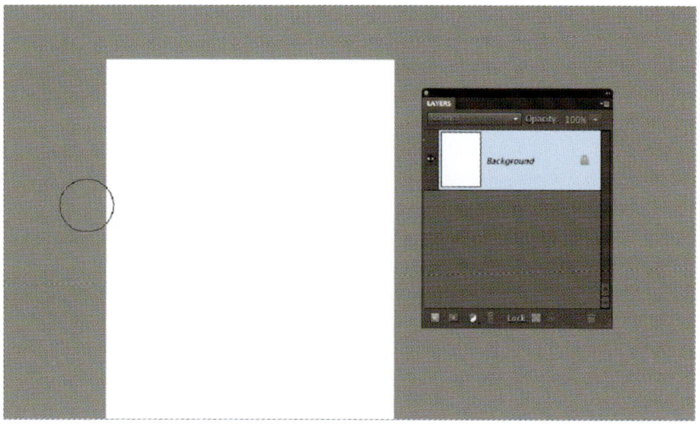

1 **START OPEN LAYERS.** In Photoshop or Elements, open the image called *LAYERS_EXAMPLE*.jpg, then bring the *Layers palette* up on screen using *Window→Layers*. Within the Layers palette you'll see a single Layer called *Background* and this is how all JPEG images will appear when opened. Of course, in this case it's a plain white background, but normally it'll be a photo.

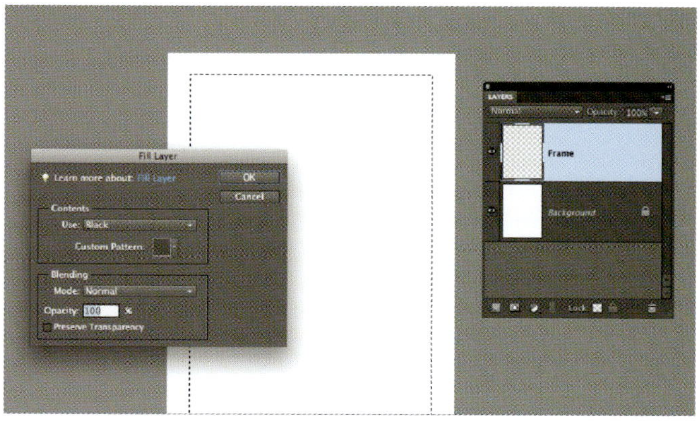

2 **MAKE A NEW LAYER.** Now go to *Layer→New Layer...* When prompted, call it *Frame* and click *OK*. An empty Layer will appear in the palette. Now pick the *Rectangular Marquee tool* and drag out a square shape. Go to *Edit→Fill Selection...* and under *Contents* choose *Black*. Click *OK* to fill the square with it. Now in the *Layers palette* you'll see the black frame above the *Background* Layer.

3 **ADD ANOTHER LAYER.** Now go to *Layer→New→Layer* and this time call it *Edge*. Pick the *Brush tool* and press *D* then *X* to set the Foreground colour to *White*. Click the *Brush Presets* drop-down in the Options bar and double-click on one of the arty brushes, then run it around the edge of the black frame. This will create a distressed look.

4 **EDIT THE LAYERS.** Within the Layers palette, click on the *Frame* Layer to highlight it (it will turn a different colour or shade to the others, showing it's active). Now go to *Filter→Blur→ Gaussian blur* and input a Radius of around *100px*. Click OK and you'll see how, because the pixels are on a separate Layer, the *Frame* Layer blurs, but the *Edge* Layer doesn't.

5 **DUPLICATE THE LAYER.** Click back on the *Edge* Layer in the *Layers palette*, then go to *Layer→New→Layer via copy*. You'll now have four Layers in the palette, with the *Edge copy* Layer at the top. Go to *Image→Rotate→Rotate Layer 180°* and the new Layer will be swung around. Next, in the Layers palette, click and drag the *Opacity* slider to around *50%*.

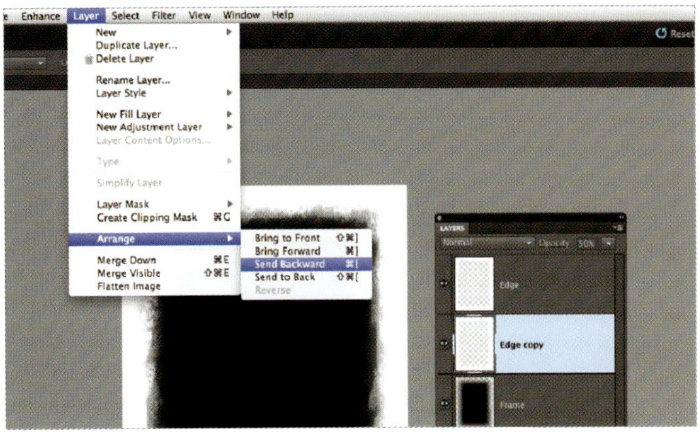

6 **REARRANGE THE LAYERS.** Now, still in the Layers palette, click on the *Edge copy* Layer, and drag it down below the *Edge* Layer. Release the mouse button and it'll drop down the Layer stack (or go to *Layer→Arrange→Send Backward*. Now press *Ctrl+T* and drag the corner handles inwards to make this Layer smaller, and let the grey areas show inside the frame. Click the tick to finish.

7 **LINK THE LAYERS.** In the Layers palette, click on the *Edge* Layer, then hold the *Shift* key and click on the *Frame* Layer - this will highlight the top three Layers in the palette. Now click on the *Link Layers* icon at the foot of the palette and you'll see link icons next to all the Layers except the *Background*. Press *Ctrl+T* and you'll be able to resize all three at the same time.

8 **FINISH ADD YOUR PHOTO!** Now the frame effect is complete, go to *Layer→Flatten image*. Open a photo you want to use within it (here we've used *BLOSSOM.jpg* from the disc), then go to *Select→All* and *Edit→Copy*. Back on the frame, go to *Edit→ Paste* and then, in the Layers palette, change Layer 1's Blending Mode to *Screen*. Finally, go to *Layer→Flatten Image* and you're done.

EXPERT ADVICE SAVING IMAGES WITH LAYERS

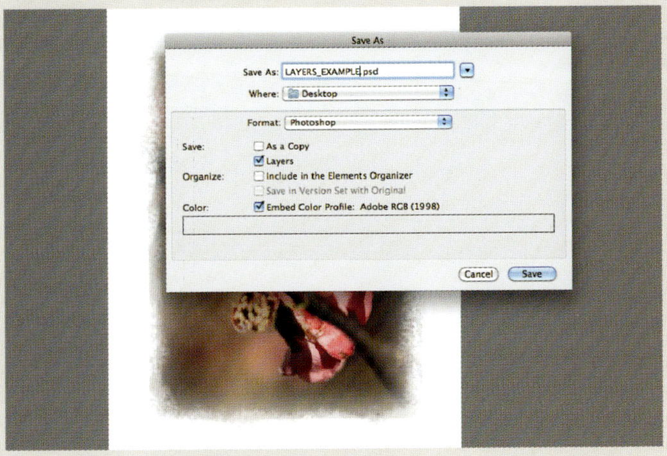

Once you add Layers to an image, it's important that you save it in the right way. If you don't, the next time you open it you'll be back to a single Background Layer.

To retain the separate Layers you've added, go to *File→ Save As...* and when prompted, choose to save the picture as a *Photoshop* (or *.psd*) file when prompted for the Format. Also, make sure that the box marked *Layers* is ticked (if you untick it you'll get a warning prompt).

Most of the time, Layered documents will default to saving as PSD files, but it doesn't hurt to check this as you save, especially as, if you try to record a Layered picture as a JPEG file you'll lose all of the Layers that you've added. You can also retain Layers by saving your image as a TIFF file (again making sure that *Layers* is ticked).

The only thing to watch out for is the size of the files you're creating. PSD and TIFF files take up a lot more disk space than JPEGs, so only save that way if you need to.

THE FINAL IMAGE
We've darkened the sky and added a foreground rock to this scene, and achieved both by using Layer Masks.

VIDEO LESSON ON THE COVER DISC!

Ps Pse

LAYER MASKING

DISCOVER HOW YOU CAN HIDE AND REVEAL PARTS OF YOUR LAYERS USING THIS SUPERB METHOD

THE START IMAGES

FILENAME SOUTHLANDING.JPG & BEACHROCK.JPG Both our start images can be found on our free disc, so you can try out Layer Masking for yourself.

BUILT INTO PHOTOSHOP and Elements 9 is a wonderful feature called *Layer Masks*. These are a special 'extra' that can be attached to a Layer in the *Layers palette*, and they can be used to hide or reveal different parts of the Layer they're associated with.

If, for example, you want to add something from one picture to another – a person, a foreground rock, a new sky – then all you do is drag it in and paint out the parts of the image you don't want.

You can, of course, do this removal work by using the *Eraser tool* and simply rubbing out the pixels, but if you want a bit more control then a Layer Mask is the way to go.

The beauty of Layer Masking is that you can restore the parts you've removed at any point, so you can change your mind and put stuff back after you've removed it!

Black & white

When it comes to using Layer Masks, it couldn't be simpler – after you've added the Mask, all you have to do is paint black into it to hide areas of a Layer, or paint white to reveal them. You can also use grey for a translucent effect, if that's the look you require.

Now follow the step-by-step below with the start images from the disc, and start using Layer Masks for real!

Masks are special attachments to a Layer. The black areas allow the Layer beneath to show through.

WITH LAYER MASKING YOU CAN RESTORE THE PARTS YOU'VE REMOVED AT ANY POINT SO YOU CAN CHANGE YOUR MIND...

1 **START OPEN YOUR IMAGE.** Open *SOUTHLANDING.jpg* into Photoshop or Elements 9. Only Elements 9 (and the full Photoshop) feature Layer Masks so Elements 8 or earlier versions can't be used for this technique. Once it's up on screen, go to *Window→Layers* to bring your *Layers palette* into view, and drag the *Background* Layer over the *Create a New Layer* icon to copy the Layer.

2 **DARKEN THE SKY.** In the *Layers palette*, click where it says *Normal* and change the Blending Mode to *Multiply*. Click on the *Add Layer Mask* icon and a white rectangle will appear alongside the Layer thumbnail. Select the *Brush tool* and choose a large, soft-edged brush. You can adjust brush size with the square brackets keys and brush softness with *Shift* and the square brackets.

3 **MASK THE SKY.** Check that the foreground colour is black (hit *D* then *X* if it's not) and then paint into the foreground of the image. You'll see the original contrast show through from the Layer beneath as you paint, because the black part of the Mask is hiding the effects of the *Multiply* Blending Mode. Continue until you have a strip of dark sky at the top that's nicely blended in with the soft brush.

4 **PASTE IN A FOREGROUND.** Now you've used your first Layer Mask, it's time to try something more difficult. Open *BEACHROCK.jpg* and when it's up, hit *Ctrl+A* to select the whole image and *Ctrl+C* to copy it to memory. Now hit *Ctrl+W* to shut it down, and when you can see your image on screen, hit *Ctrl+V* to paste it in. Sorry about all those shortcuts, but they make light work of this process!

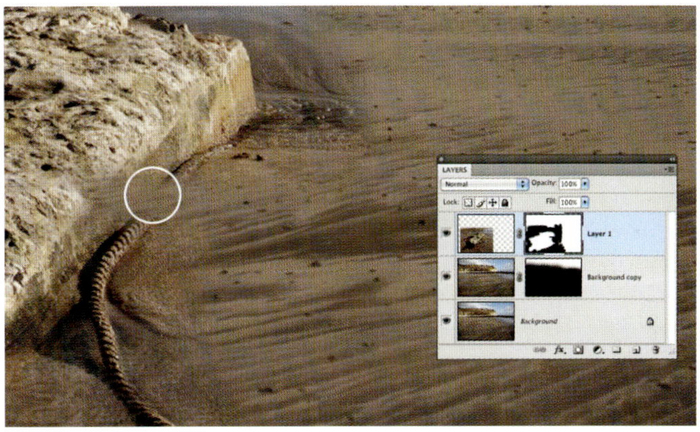

5 MASK THE FOREGROUND. Use the *Move tool* to place the foreground roughly into position, then add a Layer Mask and paint black into the area surrounding the rock. Use a smaller brush as you get nearer to the rock, the rope and the shadows cast by them, and take your time to make a detailed Mask around the items. If it helps, reduce the *Opacity* of the brush to *50%* for more control.

6 CORRECT MISTAKES ON THE FLY. If you go wrong and paint over an area you didn't intend to, just hit *X* to swap the foreground colour to White and paint over the error to restore it. The great thing about Layer Masks is you can do this whenever you like provided you save all your Layers, so if you spot a mistake further down the line, you can simply paint into your mask to fix it.

7 FINE-TUNE THE SIZE AND POSITION. Once you're happy with your Mask, you can adjust the size and shape of the rock. Provided the 'chain' link icon is visible between the Layer thumbnail and the Mask, then any changes will apply to both, so click first on the Layer thumbnail to make it active, and then hit *Ctrl+T* to enter *Free Transform* mode. Pull the 'handles' to adjust the foreground rock.

8 FINISH CHECK AND SAVE. Hit *Enter* when you're happy, and if you find you need to further refine the Mask after moving the rock, simply click on it first (it'll be surrounded by a black rectangle to show it's active) and then paint Black or White into it. When you're happy, save your work as a PSD file and all the Layers and Layer Masks will be kept, so you can drop back in at any time to adjust them.

EXPERT TIPS WHAT IF YOU DON'T HAVE LAYER MASKS?

Anyone with a full version of Photoshop will have the tools to use Layer Masks, but for Elements users, Layer Masking facilities only began with version 9 of the package. If you're using Elements 8 or earlier, you'll have Masks attached to any Adjustment Layers you create (see page 46), but you can't just add a Mask to any Layer as we show in the example above.

Though there is a way to create a Layer Masking-style facility in Elements 8 and earlier, it's a rather cumbersome process, and most users will prefer to let the *Eraser tool* stand in instead. To use the Eraser, just select it, and change the brush size and hardness as with any other brush. Work slowly and systematically, and if you make a mistake, correct it immediately by hitting *Ctrl+Z*. This will undo your last action, so all you have to do is redo the step again.

You don't get the flexibility that Masks offer, but you can still get the job done until you upgrade to the latest version.

ADJUSTMENT LAYERS

MAKE CHANGES TO YOUR PICTURES AND GET ALL THE FLEXIBILITY YOU NEED...

VIDEO LESSON ON THE COVER DISC!

Ps Pse

DOWN AT THE bottom of the *Layers palette*, there's a half black/half white icon which launches a very special type of Layer called an *Adjustment Layer*. In Elements, it gives 11 options, and in Photoshop, there are an extra 7 choices, giving a total of 18. These Adjustment Layers echo many of the commonly-used commands in Photoshop's *Image→ Adjustments* menu (or Elements' *Enhance→Adjust Lighting/Adjust Color* menus), such as *Brightness/ Contrast, Levels, Hue/Saturation* and the like.

Whereas the menu-driven commands work by permanently changing the pixels, the great thing about the Adjustment Layer options is that they allow you to make changes without affecting the pixels. What's more, the changes are not permanent, so at any point along your image-editing journey you can jump back into your Adjustment Layer and alter the settings you've made - or even remove it completely. This flexibility means that Adjustment Layers never damage your image, and it also means that you're free to change your mind and adjust effects that are too subtle or too harsh as your image develops.

We learned about Layer Masks in the last technique, and the wonderful thing about Adjustment Layers is that they have a Mask built in. This means you can hide or reveal the effects of the changes you make simply by painting white or black into the Mask. This again gives tremendous flexibility, and because nothing is fixed, it's easy to see why Layer Masks are so popular with more experienced users of Photoshop.

Now we have a rough idea of what they offer, let's put it all into practice and see how Adjustment Layers can benefit your pictures.

THE START IMAGE

FILENAME BIGBURY.JPG This pic is a great candidate for a fun, colour popping effect as the bucket, spade and colourful clothing will stand out really well against a mono background.

ADJUST THE BACKGROUND

To make the child and toys really stand out, we're going to turn the sand-and-sky setting to black & white.

POPPING THE COLOUR

If we mask out the changes we make to the image, we can leave the original colour in the subject to show through.

SAVING ADJUSTMENT LAYERS

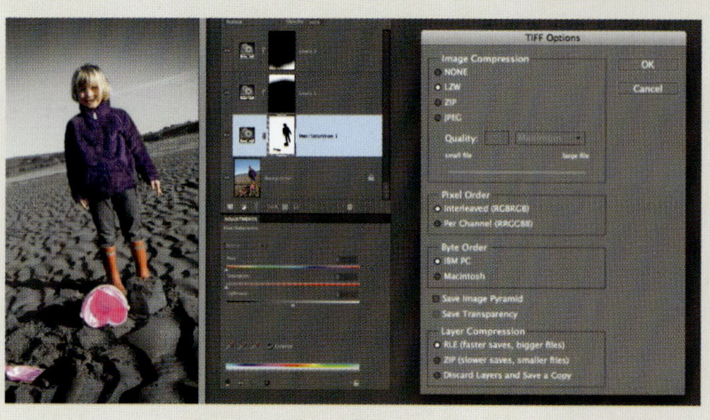

The flexibility of Adjustment Layers is the thing that makes them so popular, and provided you save them in the right format, this never changes. The format most people will choose to save all their Adustment Layers with an image is the native Photoshop *.PSD* format. This is the one we'd recommend, though if you need to save a bit of disk space, you can use TIFF as well - go to *File→ Save as...* and select *TIFF* in *Format*. In the options underneath, make sure the *Layers* box is ticked, and when you're presented with the next dialog box of options, choose *LZW* as the compression format, maximum compatibility, and choose *Interleaved* in *Pixel Order* and *RLE* in *Layer Compression*. This will give you a smaller on-disc filesize and retain all your Adjustment Layers.

THE FINAL IMAGE
Using Adjustment Layers, we've removed the colour from the background to give a fun-filled popping colour effect.

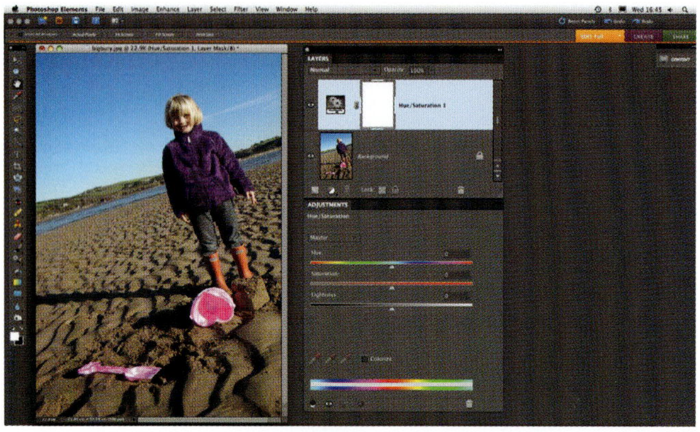

1 **START CREATE AN ADJUSTMENT LAYER.** Open up *BIGBURY.jpg* into Photoshop or Elements. Now open the *Layers palette* (*Window→Layers*) and click on the *Create New Fill or Adjustment Layer* icon (the half black/half white circle). A drop-down list of all your options will appear, and in this example we'll select *Hue/Saturation*. Click on this and the *Hue/Sat palette* will appear.

2 **CONVERT TO B&W.** To make a big change, move the *Saturation* slider all the way to the left. This will remove all the colour, making a rough-and-ready mono conversion. Click *OK* to this in older versions, or if there's no *OK* button, just leave the palette on screen. In the *Layers palette*, you can now switch the Adjustment Layer on and off using the eye icon, to see the 'before' and 'after' versions.

3 **POP THE COLOUR.** Pick up a brush and check that the foreground colour swatch is set to Black. If it's not, press *D* and then *X*. Adjust brush size using the square brackets and adjust brush hardness using *Shift* and the square brackets. Once you have a soft brush around *200px* in size, paint over the spade, bucket and girl to reveal the original colour from the Layer beneath.

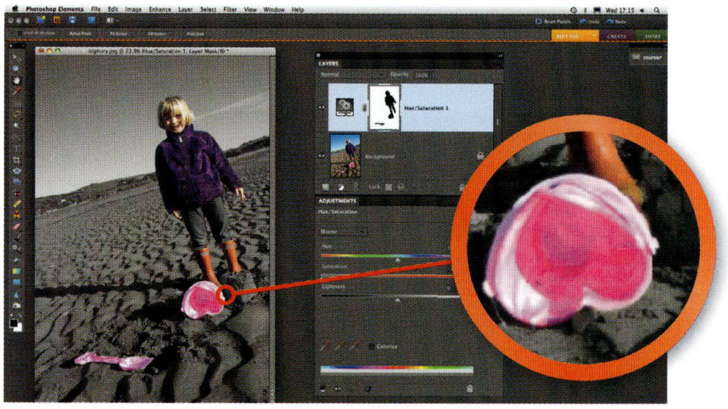

4 **PAINT YOUR MASK.** Adjust the brush size according to the size of the subject, and don't worry too much if you go over the edge or get it wrong. To correct any mistakes, simply hit *X* to swap the colours and get White as the foreground colour, and then paint over the error. Hit *X* again to go back to Black and carry on as before, painting around the subjects to bring the colour through.

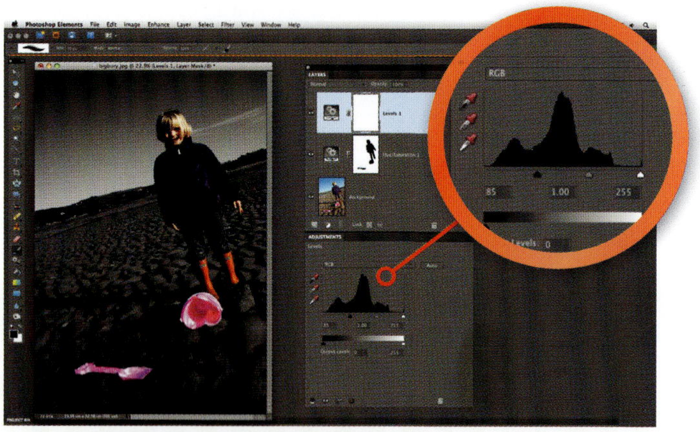

5 **ADJUST THE LEVELS.** When you've completed your mask and the popping colour effect is as perfect as you need it to be, click on the *Adjustment Layer* icon again and this time select *Levels* from the list. In the *Levels palette*, move the Black and Grey sliders to the right to darken the entire image.

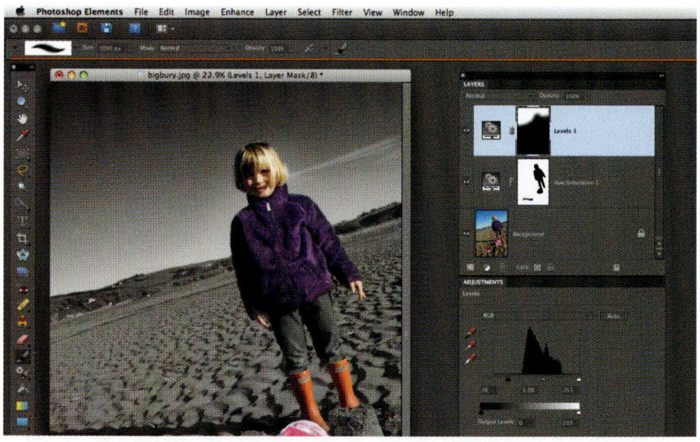

6 **DARKEN THE SKY.** Pick up a brush and after setting the foreground colour to White, set a very large, soft-edged brush around *1000px* in size. Paint into the lower two-thirds of the image to reveal the colour-popped subject and background, but leave a strip at the top to beef up the contrast in the sky and help hem in the image. Click *OK* if you can, or just leave the palette on screen.

7 **DARKEN THE FOREGROUND.** Create another *Levels* Adjustment Layer and darken the image again, this time focusing solely on the foreground area in front of the bucket and spade. Click *OK* (if you can) once it looks about right, and paint out the rest of the image as you did in the previous step, only this time just leave the affected strip at the bottom.

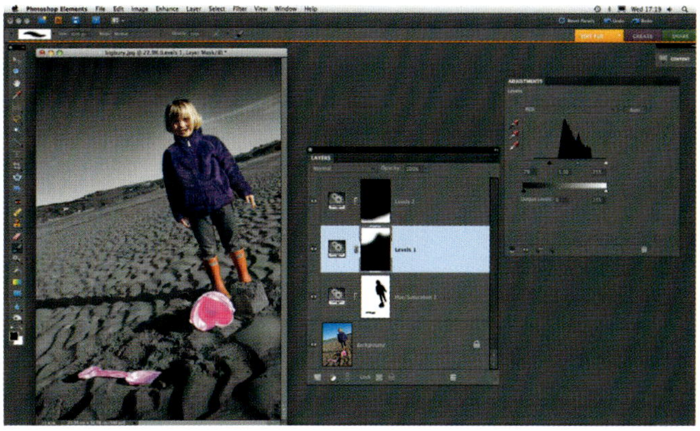

8 **FINISH CHECK YOUR WORK.** Now the pic's complete, go through your Adustment Layers. Clicking on their thumbnails in the *Layers palette* (double-clicking in older versions) will bring the adjustments up on screen with the current settings, and if you want to change them, just move the sliders. You can also fine-tune Masks with a black or white brush, so none of the creative work you've done is fixed.

TIPS FOR USING ADJUSTMENT LAYERS

Getting to grips with Adjustment Layers is very easy, as it doesn't really feel any different to using items from the *Image →Adjustments* menu in Photoshop or the *Enhance→Adjust menus* in Elements. There are a few tips which will come in handy, though, and you can use these as your experience and confidence grows.

TIP 1 Checking the Mask is selected

It's possible to have the Adjustment Layer thumbnail rather than its associated Mask selected, so before you start to paint black or white into a Mask to edit it, quickly check that it's actually highlighted in the *Layers palette*. If it is, it'll be surrounded by a black frame, so click on it to make sure.

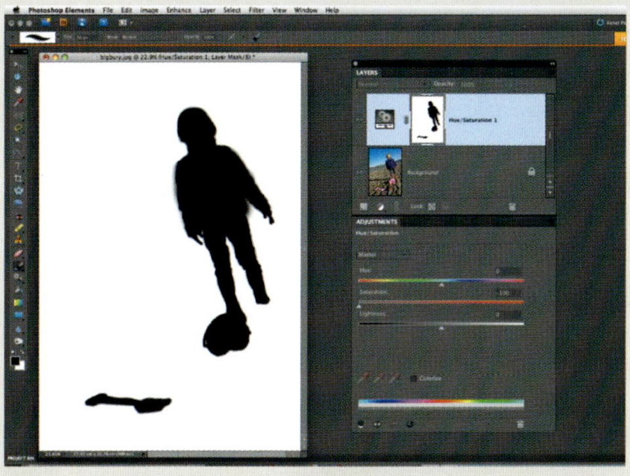

TIP 2 Viewing your Masks

Sometimes it can be hard to see how accurate your Adjustment Layer Masks are, so there's a neat trick built in to Photoshop & Elements which allows you to view the Mask image on its own. Just hold down the *Alt* key and click on the Layer Mask thumbnail to see it and even work on it alone.

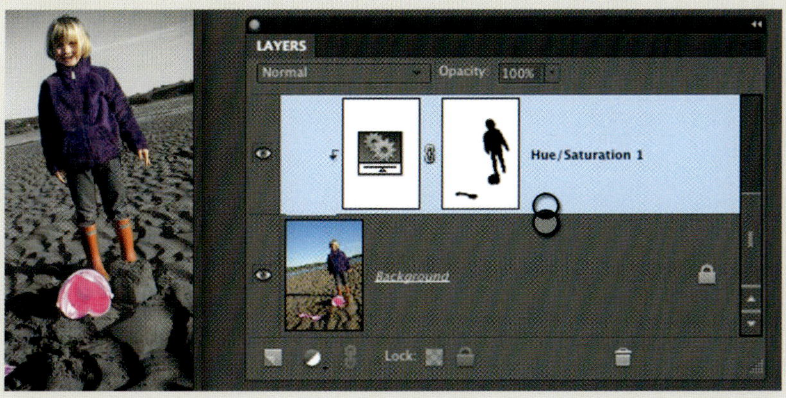

TIP 3 Clipping Adjustment Layers

Adjustment Layers affect the visible parts of all the Layers underneath them in the Layers stack. However, if you want an Adjustment Layer to apply only to the Layer immediately beneath, you have to 'clip' the Layers together.

To do this, hold the *Alt* key and hover over the line between the Adjustment Layer and the Layer beneath until the 'interlocking circles' icon appears. Once you see it, click on the line and the Layer Mask will jump to the right, and a right-angled arrow will appear. This indicates that the Layers are clipped together. To go back to normal and unclip the Layers, just repeat the exercise.

USE BLENDING MODES FOR ARTY EFFECTS

VIDEO LESSON ON THE COVER DISC!

Ps Pse

LEARN HOW TO MIX ONE LAYER WITH ANOTHER AND YOU'LL OPEN THE DOOR TO A WORLD OF CREATIVE IMAGES

THOUGH YOU CAN merge Layers in a basic way using the *Opacity* slider within the *Layers palette*, if you want to get more creative effects you need to start using Blending Modes.

Blending Modes control how a Layer interacts with the one below it and it's possible to apply all sorts of exciting styles to your pictures once you start experimenting with them. When you add a new Layer to the image you're working on, it will default to the *Normal* Blending Mode, which is effectively the 'off' setting for Layer blending. Click where it says *Normal* though and you'll reveal a list of the Blending Modes on offer and all you need to do to apply one of them is click on its name. Simple!

What's more, a Layer's Blending Mode can be changed as many times as you like and you can try out multiple effects before deciding on the one you like without damaging your pictures. Blending Modes can also be applied to Adjustment Layers, so there's no end of creative ways you can use them.

Creative blending

There are over 20 Blending Modes available in Photoshop and Elements and these are collected into six groups: Normal, Darken, Lighten, Contrast, Invert and Colour. It's the Darken, Lighten and Contrast groups that are used most commonly and one of the most effective ways to use them is to apply texture effects to your pictures. That's what you'll learn how to do in this lesson, so to follow along, make sure you load up the example pictures, *ORFORD.jpg* and *PEELING.jpg* from the disc so you can practise the technique.

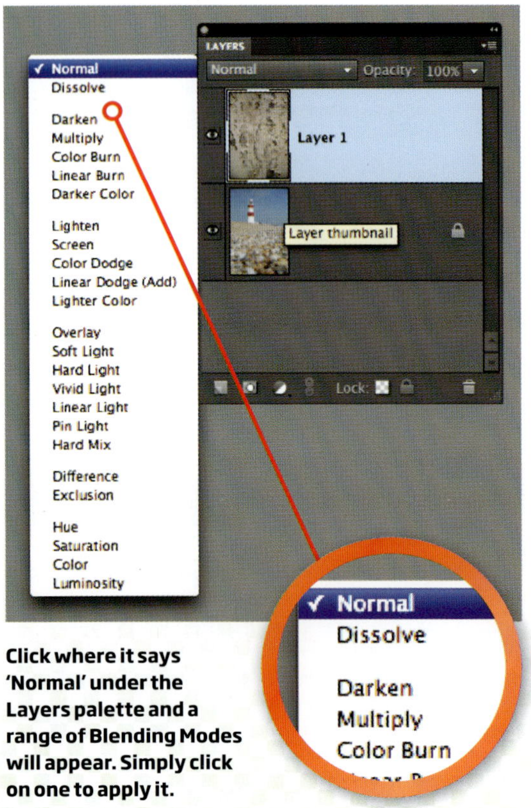

Click where it says 'Normal' under the Layers palette and a range of Blending Modes will appear. Simply click on one to apply it.

THE START IMAGES

FILE NAMES ORFORD.JPG & PEELING.JPG
The two images we used here are included on the disc free with this book and are designed for you to use while following through the technique step by step. Once you're happy with it, try it on your own images.

THE FINAL IMAGE
We added a peeling paint texture effect to our Orford Ness lighthouse pic using Layers & Blending Modes.

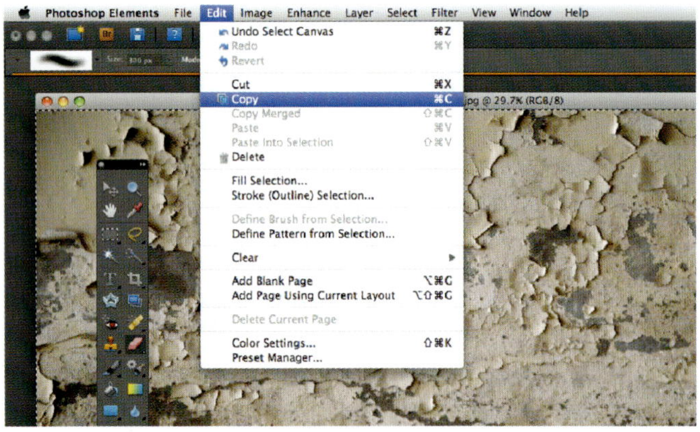

1 **START COPY THE TEXTURE.** In Photoshop or Elements, go to *File→Open* and load the picture called *PEELING.jpg* from the disc. This is the texture you're going to apply to your photo. Now go to *Select→All* and then *Edit→Copy*. Close the picture and go back to *File →Open*. Load the picture called *ORFORD.jpg* or whichever picture you want to apply the texture to.

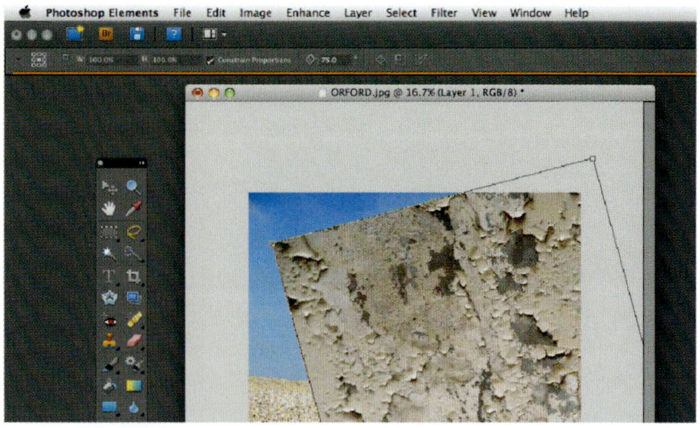

2 **PASTE THE TEXTURE.** Now go to *Edit→Paste* and the texture will drop in on top of the photo. At this stage you may need to resize or rotate the texture to fit the image. If so, press *Ctrl+T* to enter *Free Transform* mode, then drag out the corner handles to enlarge it or reduce its size. To rotate, move the cursor outside the *Transform* marquee and click and drag to spin it. Click the tick when done.

3 **CHANGE THE BLENDING MODE.** Go to *Window→Layers* to open the *Layers palette* and you'll see the texture Layer (Layer 1) sitting above the photo (the Background Layer) in the stack. Near the top of the *Layers palette*, click where it says *Normal* and the full list of Blending Modes will appear. Click on the one you want to use and it'll be applied. Here we've clicked on *Overlay*.

4 **CONTROL THE EFFECT.** Pick the *Eraser tool* then, in the Options bar, click on the *Brush Presets* window and choose a large soft-edged brush. Set its *Opacity* to *100%*, then paint over any parts of the scene where you want to hold back the effect (the lighthouse and beach). You can refine the effect using a lower opacity *Eraser*, or use a Layer Mask for more control (see page 42).

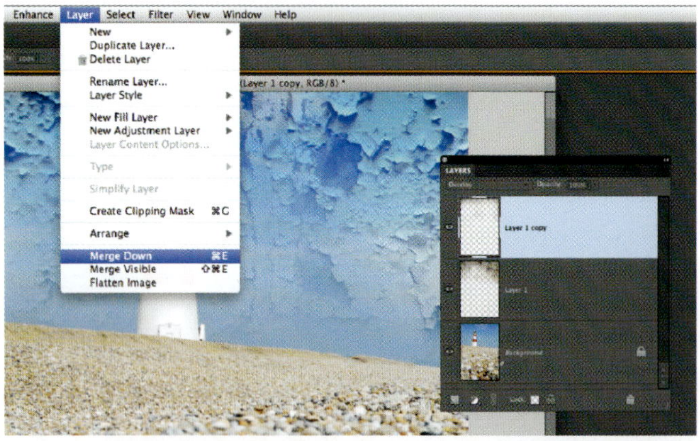

5 **STRENGTHEN THE EFFECT.** Go to *Layer→New→Layer via Copy* and the blending effect will become more intense (you'll also now have three Layers in the *Layers palette*). You can refine the new Layer further using the *Eraser tool*, or the *Opacity* slider in the *Layers palette*. Once you're happy, go to *Layer→Merge down* (or press *Ctrl+E*) and you'll go back to two Layers.

6 **ADD MORE TEXTURE.** Go to *Edit→Paste* once more and the original texture will drop back in. Resize and rotate once more if need be, then change its *Blending Mode* to *Screen*. Using the *Eraser tool* once more, delete until the effect is restricted to the lower part of the picture where it'll show up against the pebble. Go to *Layer→ New→Layer via Copy* and then *Layer→Merge down* as before.

7 ADD A TONING EFFECT. In the *Layers palette*, click on the *Create New Fill or Adjustment Layer* icon and choose *Hue/Saturation*. Click the *Colorize* box, and set the Hue to *30* and the Saturation to *15*. Back in the *Layers palette*, change the Blending Mode to *Linear Burn*. Now pick the *Brush tool* and paint black into the Adjustment Layer Mask to refine the effect.

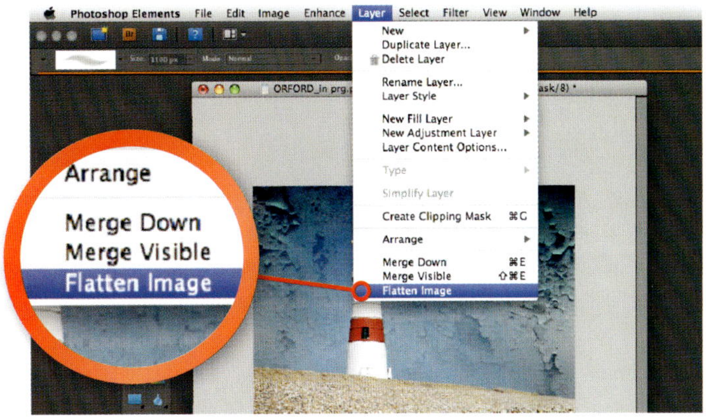

8 FINISH FLATTEN & SAVE. When you're done, you can either choose to save the file with all its Layers intact (as a *Photoshop* or *.psd* file), or you can flatten it and save it as a jpg. Go to *Layer→Flatten image*, and then to *File→Save As...* This will let you specify a new file name, so you don't end up saving over the original, untextured image. Pick *JPG* and under *Image Options* choose a quality of *Level 10* or above.

EXPERT ADVICE HOW BLENDING MODE EFFECTS VARY

When you apply a Blending Mode to a Layer, a calculation is made between the colours on the Layer below (known as the *Base colour*) and those on the Layer you're blending (known as the *Blend colour*). So if you use *Multiply* as your Blending Mode, Photoshop will multiply the Base colour by the Blend colour. Multiplying the colours will always result in a darker tone unless the Blend colour is black or white (in which case it will remain the same).

Of course you don't need to memorise what each and every Blending Mode does - it's much easier to just try them out from the list. The effects of Blending Modes aren't permanent (until you flatten the image), so experiment until you find the right one for your pic.

CREATE SUPERB COMPOSITES

USE YOUR NEWLY AQUIRED KNOWLEDGE OF LAYERS & BLEND TWO PHOTOS INTO ONE DRAMATIC IMAGE

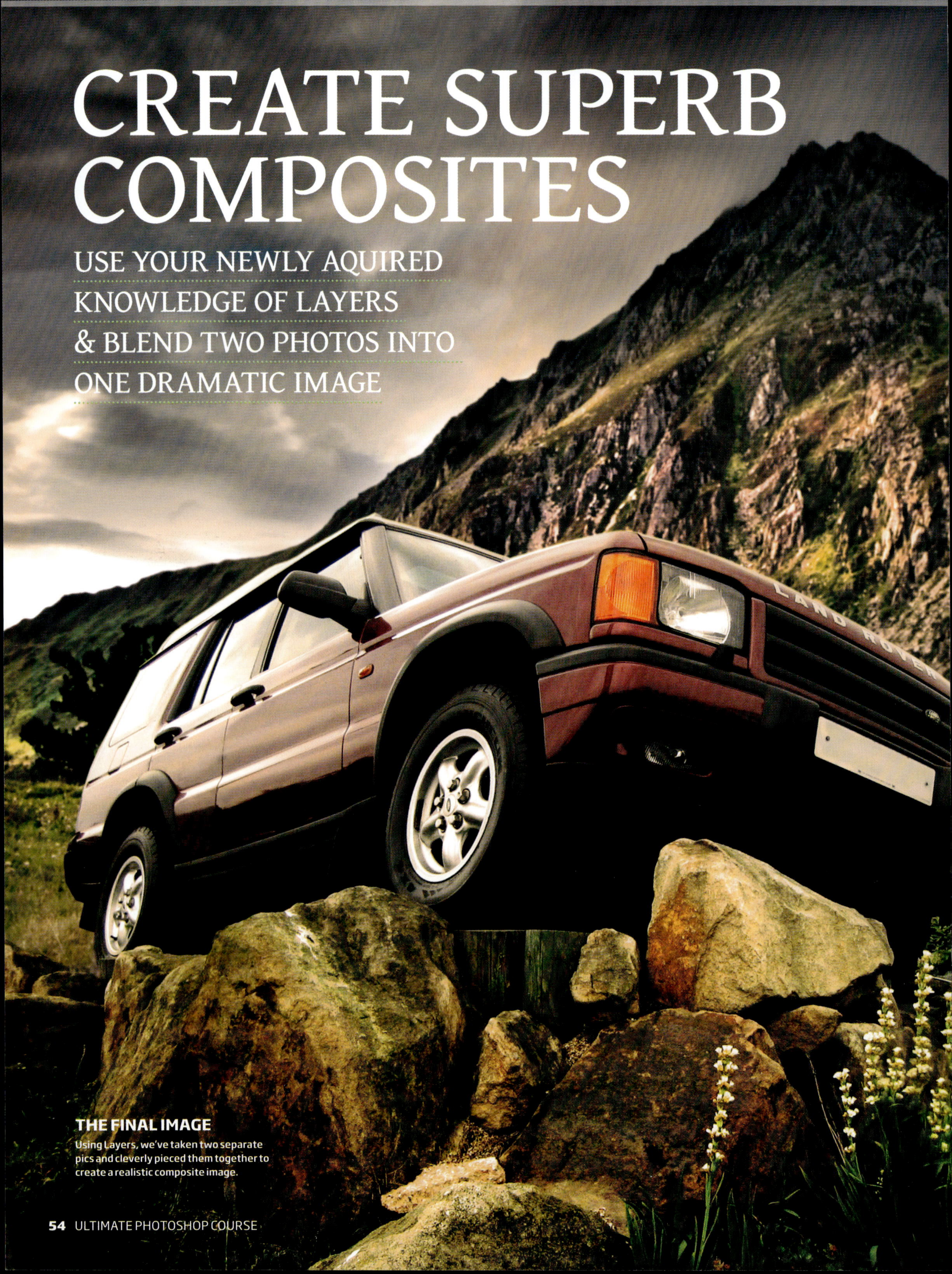

THE FINAL IMAGE

Using Layers, we've taken two separate pics and cleverly pieced them together to create a realistic composite image.

VIDEO LESSON ON THE COVER DISC!

Ps Pse

ONE OF THE MOST creative ways to use Layers is to make a composite or montage – an image that's made up from more than one photo. This might sound like something only professional image makers can do, but if you've followed the techniques in this guide you'll have all the skills you need to do it yourself.

That's right! You now know how Layers work and you've used some of the tools within the Layers palette – all you need to do to make a composite is put those skills into practice.

How to make a composite

As a photographer you want to make great images, but all the ingredients you need for this may not be present at the time of shooting. For instance you might have a great landscape scene, but one that's lacking foreground interest, or one where the sky is too bland. That's where creating a composite comes in, because you can add elements to your composition to improve it, digitally stitching them into one seamless photo. Sound daunting? It's not when you know how to use Layers!

Get creative with Layers

Composites and montages are also a great way of breathing new life into old, forgotten photos. Just dig out two or more old pictures and see what you can come up with using the following technique – you can even try out textures on your composites, as seen elsewhere in this guide.

As ever, the best way to learn is by doing, so load up the example images provided on the free disc, then move on to experimenting with your own.

NOW YOU KNOW HOW LAYERS WORK AND YOU'VE USED THE TOOLS, ALL YOU NEED TO DO TO MAKE A COMPOSITE IS PUT THOSE SKILLS INTO PRACTICE

THE START IMAGES

FILENAMES LANDROVER.JPG & MOUNTAIN.JPG The pictures we've used to create this composite can be found in the Start Images folder on the cover disc. Once you've had a go with them, try making some composites using your own snaps and see what you can cook up.

1 **START OPEN THE START IMAGES.** Open both *MOUNTAIN.JPG* and *LANDROVER.JPG* from the disc into either Photoshop or Elements. Make sure that *LANDROVER.JPG* is open in front of you by going to *Window* in the Menu bar and picking it from the bottom of the list. Now press *Ctrl+A* followed by *Ctrl+C* and switch over to *MOUNTAIN.JPG*. Press *Ctrl+V* and use the *Move tool* to reposition the Landrover at the bottom of the image.

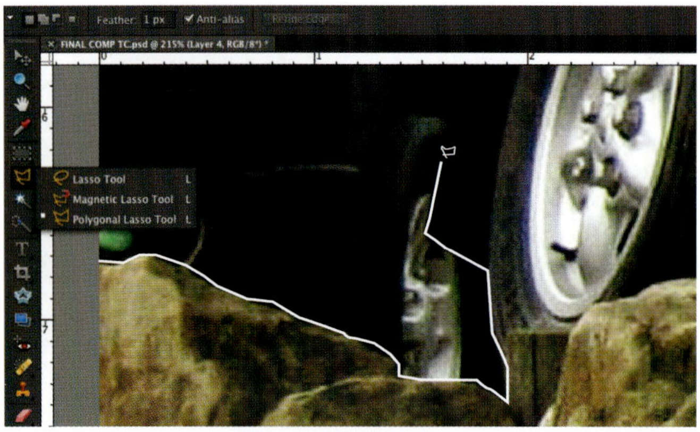

2 MASK THE LANDROVER. Grab the *Polygonal Lasso tool* (*L*) from the Toolbox and set the *Feather* to *1px*. Press *Ctrl++* a few times to zoom in and hold down the *Spacebar* to click and drag yourself into position. Starting on the left-hand side of the Landrover, carefully click around the rocks until you get all the way around the top of the vehicle and down the other side.

3 FINISH THE SELECTION. Towards the right-hand side you'll come to some plants. At this point, instead of selecting around them, just cut straight through the middle – we'll come back and neaten this up later. Complete the Selection by drawing around the edge of the frame and back to the starting point. Double-click to finish it off, then go to *Select➔Feather*, input *1px* and press *OK*.

4 MAKE A MASK. In the *Layers palette* (*Window➔Layers*) left-click on the Landrover Layer to highlight it then press the *Add Layer Mask* button at the bottom of the palette to create the mask and hide the Landrover's background from view. If you're using Elements 8 or older you won't have Layer Masks, but just skip to the panel on the opposite page for a workaround.

5 CLEAN UP THE MASK. Grab the *Brush tool* (*B*) from the Toolbox and pick a soft brush of around *100px*. Go over to the *Layers palette* and left-click on the Layer Mask that you created in the previous step to activate it. Now press *D* to return your colour palette to the default black and white and hit *X* until black is shown on top. Finally, paint over the top of the hedge to soften any harsh edges.

6 CREATE CONTRAST. Click the *Create New Fill or Adjustment Layer* button in the *Layers palette* and select *Brightness and Contrast*, then set *Contrast* to *45*. In the *Layers palette*, click and drag the newly created Adjustment Layer above the Landrover Layer. Hold down *Alt* and move the mouse inbetween the two Layers, left-clicking when you see the cursor change shape to clip them together.

7 ADD A GRADIENT. Press *Ctrl+Shift+N* to create a new Layer, hit *OK*, then choose the *Gradient tool* from the Toolbox. Go up to the *Gradient picker* in the Options bar and choose the *Black to Transparent* gradient. Holding *Shift*, left-click and drag the mouse from the bottom of the image to the tip of the rocks, then release. Finally, set the Layer *Opacity* to *50%* and the *Blending mode* to *Overlay*.

8 **WARM IT UP.** Click the *Create New Fill or Adjustment Layer* button in the *Layers palette* once again, but this time pick *Photo Filter* from the list. Make sure that the *Filter* option is set to *Warming Filter 85*, and then use the slider to increase the *Density* to *65%*. Finally, within the Layers palette, left-click and drag this new Adjustment Layer to the top of the stack.

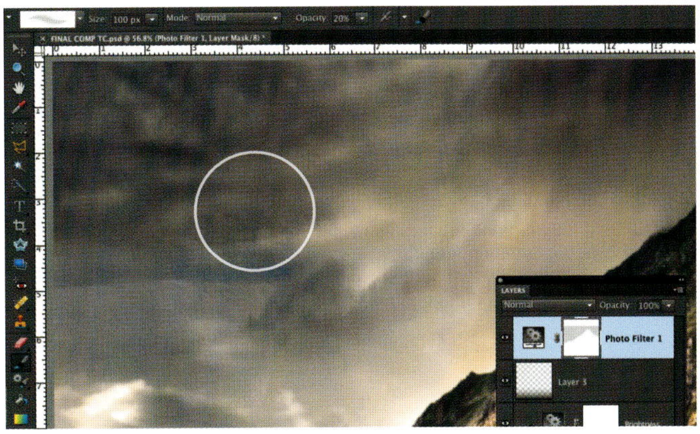

9 **FINISH RESTORE COLOUR.** Now left-click the Layer Mask next to the *Photo Filter Adjustment Layer* in the Layers palette, then grab the *Brush tool* (*B*) from the Toolbox once again, pick a soft brush of around *100px*, and set the *Opacity* to *20%*. Paint over the sky to bring back some of the blue colour. Once you're finished, don't forget to save your work by going to *File→ Save As...*

EXPERT ADVICE USING THE ERASER TOOL IN ELEMENTS

As you'll have already read in this guide, if you own a copy of Elements that's older than version 9, then the Layer Mask feature won't be available to you. But the good news is there's a simple way around it. After Step 3 of this composite tutorial, just switch to following the steps below, then resume the technique at Step 6.

A workaround with the *Eraser tool*

- **With the Landrover selected, start off by going to *Select→ Inverse* to invert the Selection so that it covers the background. Then, simply press *Backspace* on your keyboard to delete it.**
- **Now it's time to sort out the hedge section on the right-hand side of the image. Start by grabbing the *Eraser tool* from the Toolbox, then go up to the *Brush picker* in the Options bar, and choose a nice soft brush of around *100px*.**
- **Finally, go over to the hedge area on the right-hand side and zoom in slightly by pressing *Ctrl++*. Now you can carefully start to remove any hard edges – if you happen to make a mistake, undo your last step by pressing *Ctrl+Z*.**

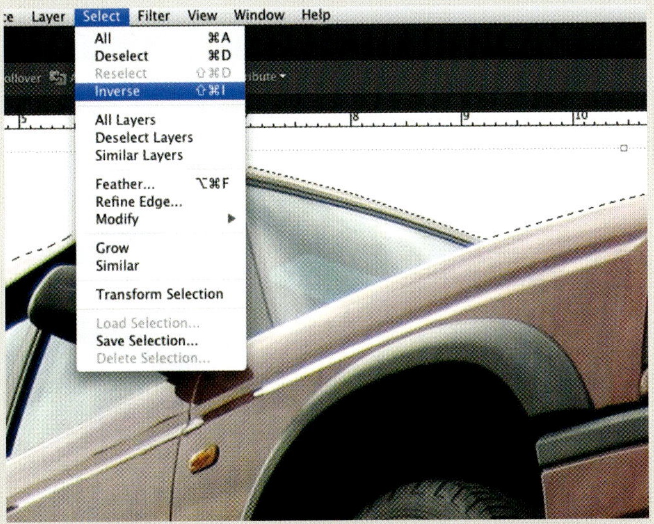

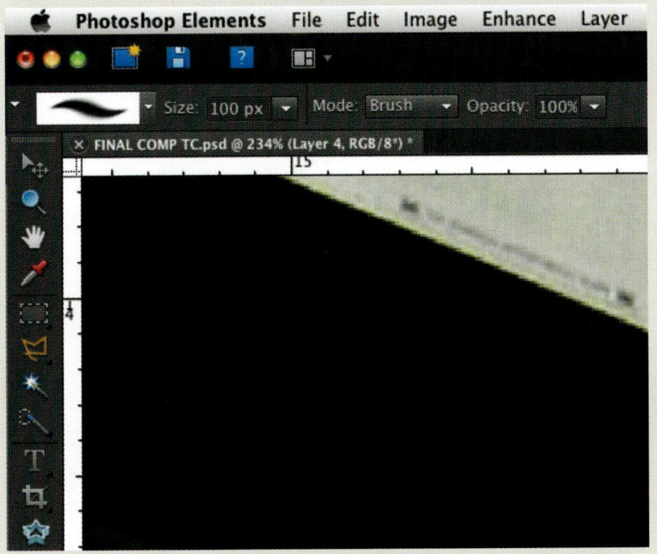

CHAPTER 3
SELECTIONS MADE SIMPLE

USE SELECTIONS & SELECTION TOOLS TO MAKE MORE OF YOUR PICS

Remember, when you see this icon, there's a video lesson of the technique on the cover DVD.

P70 EDIT QUICKLY & ACCURATELY

Learn how the ***Quick Selection tool*** works and how it can be used with ***Refine Edge*** to improve your pictures in a flash.

P66 CUT OUT BLAND SKIES FOR GOOD

The ***Magic Wand tool*** is ideal for Selecting broad areas of flat colour and that makes it perfect for replacing dull skies - give it a try!

LEARN WITH US!

SELECTIONS ARE VITAL FOR IMAGING EDITING, SO IF YOU WANT TO MAKE THE BEST OF YOUR PICS IT'S VITAL YOU KNOW HOW TO USE THEM...

P78 USE SELECTIONS TO MAKE A MULTI-PICTURE MONTAGE

We'll show you how to use the *Elliptical Marquee tool* to select different pictures and then copy them into a single image.

P64 MAKE SELECTIVE ADJUSTMENTS TO IMPROVE LIGHTING

There's rarely any point in making 'global' adjustments to landscape pics – make a Selection first and you'll be able to darken skies and lighten foregrounds with ease.

P74 PICK OUT TRICKY SUBJECTS

If you've got a complex subject that needs separating from its background, we'll show you how to cut it out with real precision using the *Polygonal Lasso tool*.

IT'S NO EXAGGERATION TO SAY THAT THE SELECTION TOOLS ARE VITAL FOR EDITING PICS!

IN THIS SPECIAL GUIDE you'll get an introduction to Selections in Photoshop and Elements, finding out what they are, the right way to use them, and most importantly how Selections can help you improve your digital pictures.

It's no exaggeration to say that, without the Selection tools, Photoshop would be a lot less useful, because by employing them in the right way you can massively expand your ability to make simple improvements to your shots. Get to know them really well and you can become even more creative, making precise cut-outs and stunning multi-image montages.

Selection tools

There are lots of ways to make a Selection in Photoshop, but essentially they all do the same thing, helping you to define an area of a picture that you're about to work on. Once the Selection is made, the part you've picked will be surrounded by dotted lines known as 'marching ants' and this means you can change the part you've Selected without affecting any other section of the picture. It can be deleted, copied, changed in size, filtered, darkened, lightened, or even transferred into an entirely new pic, so there's loads to try!

VIDEO LESSON ON THE COVER DISC!

Ps Pse

When you see this CD-ROM logo, it means there's an in-depth video lesson on our cover disc that accompanies the technique. Watch and learn as one of our experts takes you through the project, step by step!

1 HOW CAN YOU FIX THIS PICTURE?

The lighting needs to be evened up in this pic by darkening the sky and lightening the grass but unless you make a Selection, you can't fix one without

2 SELECTIVE ADJUSTMENT TO A SKY

To make a Selection of the sky, simply draw around it using the Lasso tool. Once completed, marching ants will appear, fencing off the area ready for adjustment. You can then change the lighting in just this part of the picture.

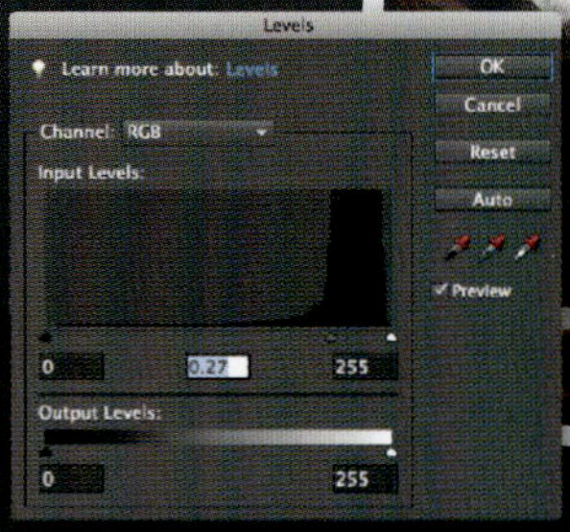

VIDEO LESSON ON THE COVER DISC!

Ps Pse

START USING SELECTIONS

IF YOU WANT TO MAKE BETTER PICTURES, USING SELECTIONS IS VITAL – HERE'S HOW THEY WORK...

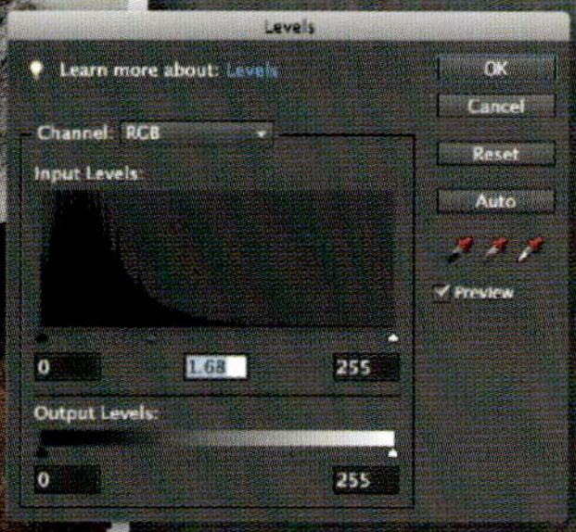

3 SELECTIVE ADJUSTMENT TO HILLSIDE

Do the same to the lower part of the picture and you can lighten it independently from the rest just the same as you darkened the sky. Feathering the Selection helps it look more natural.

4 THE FINAL ENHANCED IMAGE

With just those two simple adjustments made, the lighting in the picture is vastly improved and it's ready to show off in all its new-found glory.

SELECTIONS ARE ALL ABOUT picking which area of your image you want to improve and this means you can make accurate adjustments to specific parts of a picture, rather than applying effects to the whole thing. It's very much like using stencils or masking tape when decorating your home – the Selections you make create a barrier up to which you can work.

But making selective adjustments to photos certainly isn't a new thing – photographers have always improved pictures in this way, most commonly by covering parts of the print during the enlargement process and blocking light from reaching parts of the photo-sensitive paper to vary the exposure – a process called dodging and burning. Usually this was done with hands or improvised tools, making it a fiddly exercise.

Of course, in the digital age all of this is done in Photoshop and you can see how it works in the example pictures above. Here, Selections have been used to fence off different areas of the image prior to adjustment – in this case using the *Levels palette* to darken or lighten that part of the picture.

It's also helpful to note how, with each new Selection made, the resulting Histogram within the Levels palette changes, because it's only reading the pixels within the marching ants. So, in the pictures above, when the sky is selected the Histogram shows us the area is very light, and when the foreground is selected the opposite is true. Turn over to read more about the Selection tools and see how we've used them on this example picture...

UNDERSTANDING THE SELECTION TOOLS

There are loads of different ways to make a Selection in Photoshop or Elements and, in fact, the sheer amount of Selection tools may seem quite bewildering at first. Rest assured though, they're all in there for a reason, and each does something specific and useful, meaning whatever you need to Select in your pictures, there'll be a tool that can do the job.

The majority of the time, Selections are made using tools from within the Toolbox and you'll find an expanded view of this below, showing the options available. This may change depending on the version of Photoshop that you're running, particularly as new tools are added over time, but the core (and most useful) options are common to all versions, and those are the ones we'll look at in this guide.

> EACH TOOL DOES SOMETHING SPECIFIC & USEFUL – THEY'RE ALL THERE FOR A REASON!

Which tool to use

Once you've picked a Selection tool from the Toolbox and used it on your picture you can refine the Selection using the options under the *Select* menu at the top of the screen, like modifying its size or position, softening its edge or saving it for later use.

As for picking the right tool for the job, your options are roughly split into the tools that work manually and those that work automatically. The former, which includes the *Lasso* and *Marquee tools*, simply involve drawing around the area you want to adjust using your mouse, or dragging out a marquee over it. The automatic tools, like the *Magic Wand tool*, use the colour values of the pixels that make up your picture on which to base their Selections, so you can pick out whole areas with a single click.

Work through this guide and you'll soon see which is more suited to your way of working or the image you're editing.

EXPLAINED THE SELECTION TOOLS

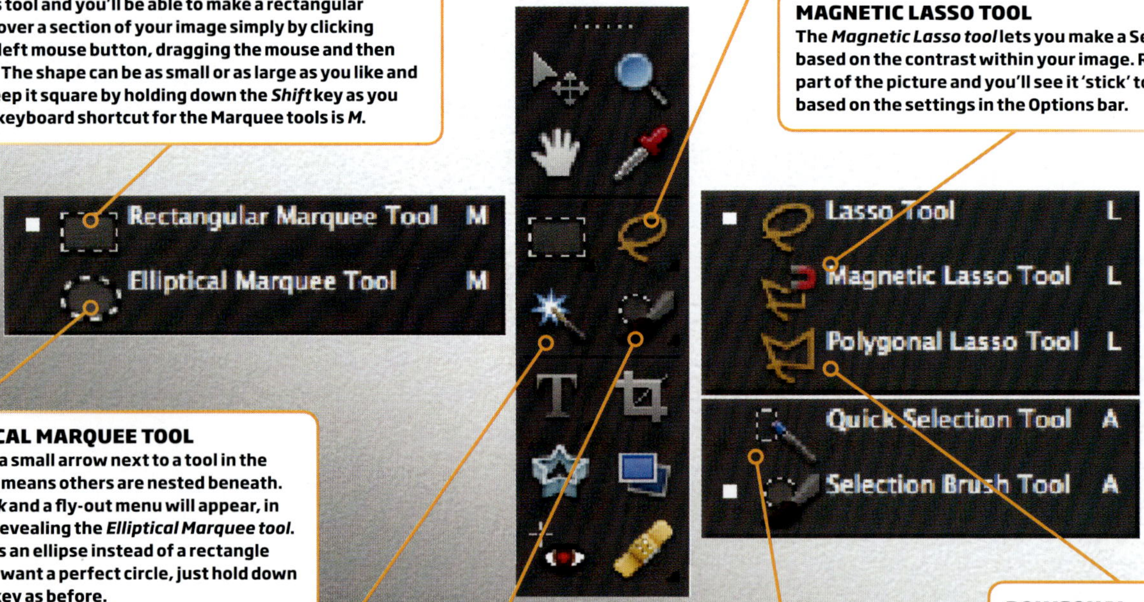

LASSO TOOL
The *Lasso tool* works just like drawing onto the image with a pencil, so it's great for making loose, sweeping, freehand Selections. For more fiddly work, though, the *Polygonal Lasso* is better. The keyboard shortcut is *L*.

RECTANGULAR MARQUEE TOOL
Select this tool and you'll be able to make a rectangular Selection over a section of your image simply by clicking with your left mouse button, dragging the mouse and then releasing. The shape can be as small or as large as you like and you can keep it square by holding down the *Shift* key as you drag. The keyboard shortcut for the Marquee tools is *M*.

MAGNETIC LASSO TOOL
The *Magnetic Lasso tool* lets you make a Selection based on the contrast within your image. Run it over part of the picture and you'll see it 'stick' to any edges based on the settings in the Options bar.

ELLIPTICAL MARQUEE TOOL
If you see a small arrow next to a tool in the Toolbox it means others are nested beneath. *Right-click* and a fly-out menu will appear, in this case revealing the *Elliptical Marquee tool*. This draws an ellipse instead of a rectangle and if you want a perfect circle, just hold down the *Shift* key as before.

POLYGONAL LASSO TOOL
A very accurate and easy-to-use Selection tool, the *Polygonal Lasso* lets you click around whatever part of the image you want to select, making even complex shapes and objects easy to adjust.

MAGIC WAND TOOL
The *Magic Wand tool* lets you select individual colours in an image using a *Tolerance* setting. Just click on any part of the picture and marching ants will appear based on your preferences in the Options bar.

SELECTION BRUSH TOOL
This functions just like a regular brush, but instead of painting in a colour, you paint a Selection. The brush can be changed in size and shape, and by applying softness to its edge you'll get a pre-Feathered Selection.

QUICK SELECTION TOOL
Functioning a bit like a real-time *Magic Wand tool*, the *Quick Selection tool* will produce an intuitive Selection wherever you apply it to the image.
Sweep it over a blue sky, for example, and the whole area will be quickly surrounded by the 'marching ants'.

STEP-BY-STEP BASIC SELECTIONS IN ACTION

When you need to make selective changes to an image, the first thing to do is decide which tool is best for the job. This will depend largely on the type of area you're selecting and what you'll be doing to the Selected area once it's ready for adjustment.

In the case of this landscape image we want to improve the lighting by darkening the sky and lightening the foreground. Both areas are probably too complex to use the automatic Selection tools, like the Magic Wand, and the Marquee tools are too rigid to deal with the tree projecting into the sky and the slope of the hillside. This brings us neatly on to the Lasso tool which will let us draw freehand over the areas we want to select.

> WHEN YOU NEED TO MAKE SELECTIVE CHANGES TO AN IMAGE FIRST DECIDE WHICH TOOL IS BEST FOR THE JOB

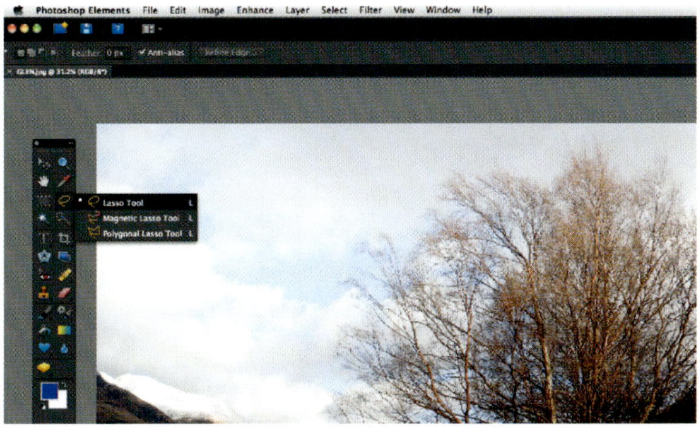

1 START PICK A SELECTION TOOL. Open the picture called *GLEN.jpg* from the cover disc and choose the *Lasso tool* from the Toolbox. This may be hiding under one of the other Lasso tools, so just press *L* to cycle through them (*Shift+L* in Photoshop), or click and hold until a fly-out list appears. In the Options bar, make sure that *New Selection* is set, *Feather* is set to *0* and *Anti-alias* is ticked.

2 DRAW A SELECTION. Press *Ctrl* and the *minus* key so there's some space around your picture, then, next to the mountain on the right, click and drag your mouse to start drawing out the Selection. Draw up over the tree, down the other side and then back around the top of the picture. When you get back to the point you started at, release the button and the 'marching ants' will appear.

3 DARKEN THE SKY. The 'marching ants' form the edges of the Selection, so only pixels inside of them will be affected by adjustments you make. Now let's soften the Selection... in the Options bar, click on *Refine Edge* and move the *Feather* slider to *250px*. Click *OK*. Finally, press *Ctrl+L* to bring up the *Levels palette*, then move the middle slider to the right. Press *OK* when you're done.

4 FINISH LAST SELECTION. After you click *OK*, go to *Select → Deselect* (*Ctrl+D*) to get rid of the 'marching ants'. Now make another Selection, this time running down the angle of the hillside and foreground. Use Refine Edge to *Feather* it as before, press *Ctrl+L* to bring up the *Levels palette* again and this time move the middle slider to the left. Press *OK*, then *Ctrl+D* and you're done.

USE SELECTIONS TO FIX BLAND SKIES

VIDEO LESSON ON THE COVER DISC!

Ps Pse

FLAT AREAS OF COLOUR CAN BE EASILY SELECTED WITH THE MAGIC WAND TOOL, HELPING YOU INJECT VITAL DETAIL

THE START IMAGES

FILE NAMES ***SPURN_POINT.JPG & SPURN_SKY.JPG***

The start images used in this technique and the accompanying video lesson can be found in the *Start Images* folder on the cover disc. Just copy them to your PC and run through the lesson, then have a go with your own images.

USING THE MAGIC WAND TOOL...

Though the *Magic Wand tool* is one of the more simple and automatic Selection tools in Photoshop and Elements, it's still a very useful one if used in the right way. The *Magic Wand tool* allows you to quickly and accurately select parts of your image using a *Tolerance* setting - a measure of its sensitivity which you can define in the Options bar from *0* to *255*.

In conjunction with its Tolerance setting the *Magic Wand tool* looks for similar colours in your image on which to base its Selection, so the more you increase the Tolerance, the more of the picture will be Selected - a low Tolerance setting will only pick out pixels very close in colour to the one you've clicked on, but a high Tolerance will do the opposite.

> THE MAGIC WAND TOOL IS A VERY USEFUL OPTION FOR SELECTING FLAT SKIES...

Cut out the sky

In practice this means that you only need to click on one part of the picture and 'marching ants' will spread out to cover all of the pixels within the range you've set. This makes the *Magic Wand tool* a very useful and speedy option for selecting large areas of colour, or similar shades in a picture - like the blue of a clear sky, as in the example picture we're using for this technique, *SPURN_POINT.jpg*.

Once that Selection is made and refined slightly using the *Select* menu you can use it to your advantage. So in this case we'll use it to remove the pixels that make up the original sky and then insert a new one. Thanks to the Selection made with the *Magic Wand tool* this will be easy and with a little tidying up it'll look great and improve the picture no end.

Make sure you check out the accompanying video lesson to see how it's all done!

1 **START OPEN THE IMAGE.** Open the picture in which you want to replace the sky (in this case *SPURN_POINT.jpg* from the cover disc), and then pick the *Magic Wand tool* from the Toolbox. In the Options bar, make sure that the Magic Wand tool's *Tolerance* is set to a low value of around 10 and that the *Contiguous* and *Anti-Alias* boxes are both ticked.

2 **MAKE THE SELECTION.** Click on the sky and 'marching ants' will appear, but they won't cover it all. Now, hold down the *Shift* key, or click on the *Add to Selection* icon in the Options bar, then click again on a part of the sky that hasn't been selected. The Selection will start to grow, so keep clicking until the whole sky is fenced in by the 'marching ants'.

3 **SELECT FINE DETAILS.** Using the *Zoom tool*, or by pressing *Ctrl* and the *Plus* key, zoom into the image and look for any small parts of the sky that haven't been selected. To add them to the Selected area, make sure the *Add to Selection* icon is still active in the Options bar, or keep the *Shift* key held as you click. Here, we've clicked between the railings on top of the lighthouse.

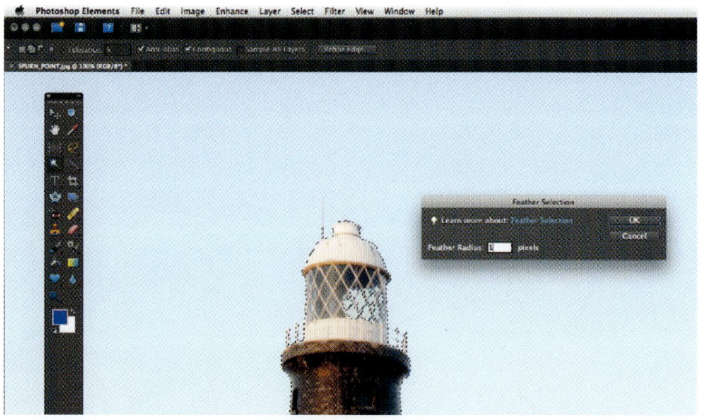

4 **MODIFY & FEATHER.** To make sure your Selection precisely follows the edge of the subject, go to *Select→ Modify→ Expand*, input *1 pixel* and then press *OK*. Then, to avoid getting too sharp an edge on the new sky you're about to add, go back to the Select menu and pick *Feather*. Here, input *0.5px* and click *OK*. Now the Selection is complete you can use it to add the sky.

5 COPY THE LAYER. Go to *Select→ Inverse* and the 'marching ants' will swap to the non-selected parts. Next, go to *Layer→ New→ Layer via copy* and then go to *Window→ Layers*. In the *Layers palette*, you'll notice that there's now a copy of the Lighthouse, but the sky has been replaced by a chequerboard effect - that's where the original sky was removed and where we'll add the new one.

6 OPEN THE SKY. In the *Layers palette*, click on the *Background* Layer and then go to *File→ Open* and load up the replacement sky image from the disc (it's called *SPURN_SKY.jpg*). On this picture, go to *Select→ All*, and then choose *Edit→ Copy*. Back on the original, go to *Edit→ Paste* and then pick the *Move tool* and roughly drag it into position.

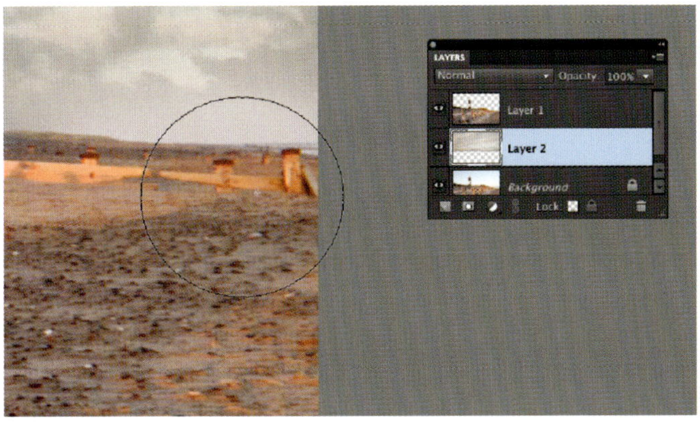

7 BLEND THE LAYERS. Depending on the image you're working on, you may need to do some blending. Next, pick the *Eraser tool* and click on the preset drop-down, choosing a 300px, soft-edged brush. In the Options bar, set the Eraser's *Opacity* to *100%* and then, making sure that Layer 2 is still highlighted in the *Layers palette*, run the *Eraser* along the horizon to improve the join.

8 FINISH FLATTEN & SAVE. Next, lower the *Opacity* of the *Eraser* to *20%* and sweep it along further above the horizon to improve the blend made by the original Selection. Finally, go to *Layer→ Flatten Image*, then File→ Save As... Call the picture *SPURN_NEW_SKY*, so you don't save over the the original and save it as a JPEG at a *Quality* of *Level 10* or above.

THE MAGIC WAND'S CONTIGUOUS OPTION

When you pick the *Magic Wand tool* from the Toolbox, the settings that govern how it makes Selections will appear in the Options bar, and one of the most important is marked *Contiguous*.

With this option *ticked*, clicking on the image will restrict your Selection to adjacent areas of colour. This means that once the Selection reaches a colour outside of its *Tolerance* range it'll stop, even though other colours within its range exist in the image. If the *Contiguous* option is *unticked*, all pixels in the entire image that are within the *Tolerance* range will be Selected.

In the examples on the left you can see that with the *Contiguous* option ticked and clicking on the blue sky, the Selection stops when it reaches the different colours of the lighthouse's railings. With the option unticked all the blues are Selected, including those between the railings, though the blues in the windows are still outside the *Tolerance* range.

USING THE QUICK SELECTION TOOL

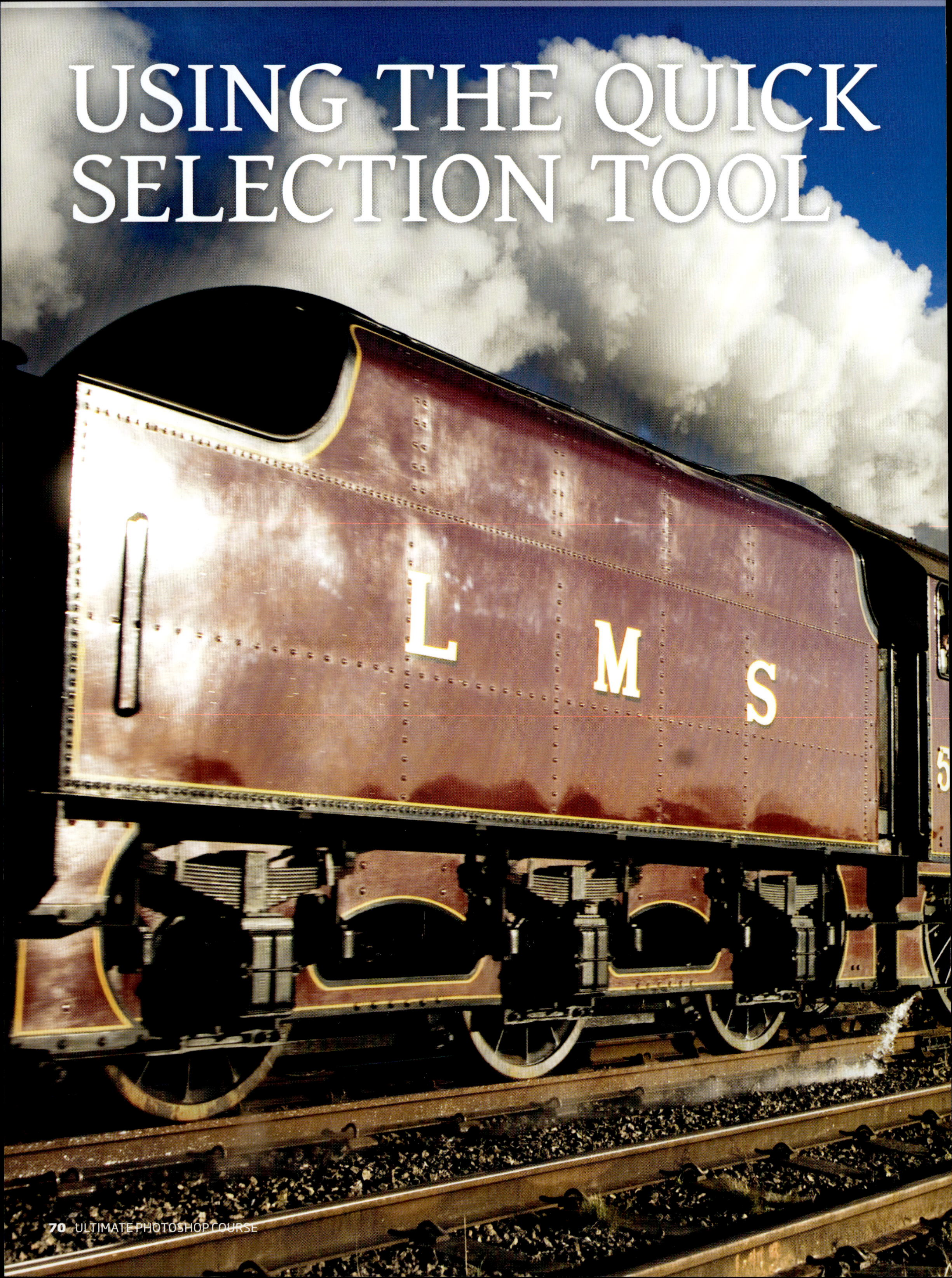

LEARN HOW TO USE THE QUICK SELECTION TOOL & MAKE FAST, ACCURATE SELECTIONS

SOME OF THE Selection tools can take time to master, but nothing could be further from the truth when it comes to the *Quick Selection tool*. It's designed to take the hassle out of making Selections and speed up the time it takes to work around the areas of a picture you'd like to edit.

Using it is very much like painting with one of Photoshop's brush tools, the real difference being that the area you paint is the area that ultimately ends up being part of your Selection. It's an intuitive tool that's capable of working out where the edges are in your images and this helps it to pick out subjects automatically, even if they're made up of different colours, which gives it an advantage over the *Magic Wand tool*. Here we'll use it to make separate Selections of the sky, steam engine and foreground ready to edit. To see how easy it is to use,follow our simple step-by-step over the page and watch the video tutorial on the cover disc.

VIDEO LESSON ON THE COVER DISC!

Ps Pse

THE START IMAGE

FILE NAMES
JUBILEE.JPG
For our main image we've used this shot of a steam engine powering into the distance. We used the *Quick Selection tool* to help us select the three key areas of the shot - the sky, the locomotive and the foreground, before enhancing these areas using Adjustment Layers.

1 **START OPEN THE IMAGE TO EDIT.** Locate the file *JUBILEE.jpg* on the disc and open it into Photoshop or Elements. From the Toolbox, select the *Quick Selection tool*. In the Options bar at the top of the screen, make sure you have *New Selection* highlighted and beside this click the *Brush Picker* and set the *Size* or *Diameter* to *250px*. Finally make sure that *Auto Enhance* is **not** ticked.

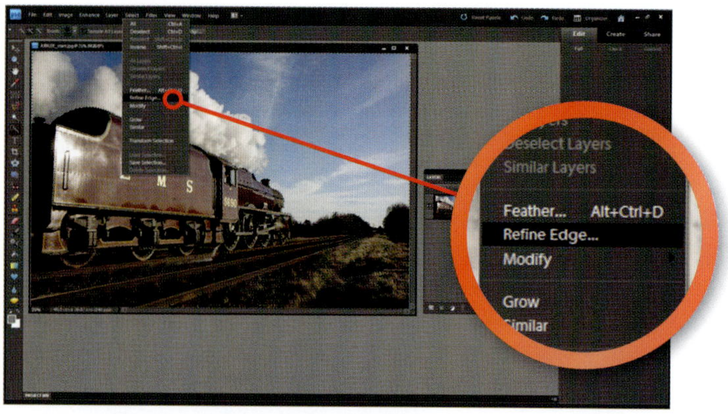

2 **WORK THROUGH THE SKY AREA.** Click on the sky and slowly drag the tool from right to left. You'll notice how the 'marching ants' run around the front of the train and above the trees. Continue to the left so the steam is included in the Selection. Now open the *Refine Edge* dialog by going to *Select → Refine Edge*. Alternatively, click on the *Refine Edge* button in the Options bar.

3 **SOFTEN THE SELECTION EDGE.** Drag the *Feather* slider to the right, setting it to *15px* before hitting *OK*. Now go to *Layer → New Adjustment Layer → Levels*. To enrich the sky and make the blue tones more vivid, drag the *Shadows* slider right to a value of *56* and drag the *Highlights* slider left to *240*. Hit *OK* or exit the palette. Before moving on, check the *Quick Selection tool* is still picked.

4 **SELECT THE TRAIN.** Run the *Quick Selection tool* from left to right over the train and down as far as the rails. Your Selection should hug the outline of the train, but if the Selection runs into an area that you don't want it to, move into the Options bar and select the *Subtract from Selection* icon. Use a smaller *100px* brush and run the tool beneath the edge of where you'd like the Selection to be.

5 **BOOST THE RED TONES.** Open *Refine Edge* again and set the *Feather* to *15px* to soften the Selection. Hit *OK*. Go to *Layer → New Adjustment Layer → Hue/Saturation* and increase the *Saturation* to *+40* to brighten the red tones of the train. Hit *OK*. Now run the *Quick Selection tool* through the foreground area to select the tracks underneath the locomotive's wheels and the distant trees.

6 **FINISH BRIGHTEN THE FOREGROUND.** Open *Refine Edge* again, and this time use a larger *50px* Feather to create a gradual blend between the selected and non-selected areas. Hit *OK*. Add an *Adjustment Layer* as before, this time picking *Levels*. Drag the white point slider left to brighten the foreground, then exit or press *OK*. Finally, you can save the image by going to *File → Save As*.

USE SELECTIONS FOR PRECISE CLONING WORK

If there's a distraction in one of your images that's difficult to remove without damaging nearby pixels, you'll need to use a Selection to 'fence off' the area you're intending to work around.

Making a Selection will work much like a barrier, preventing any bleeding or smudging when you're using the Cloning and Healing tools so it's really helpful for preserving the outlines of any distinctive details in your shots.

In the start image *JUBILEE.jpg*, there's a distracting telegraph pole above the locomotive's chimney. While it'd be easy enough to use the *Clone Stamp tool* to sample new pixels and brush up against the chimney, there's a risk of damaging its edge, as shown in the image, above left.

A much better and more precise way of working is to 'ring' the loco's chimney first with a Selection, using the *Lasso tool* or *Polygonal Lasso tool*. Draw around the chimney, then get the inverse of the Selection (*Select→ Inverse*) so everything except the chimney is selected. When this has been done you can pick the *Clone Stamp tool* from the Toolbox, then hold the *Alt* key and click on a clean part of the sky to sample the pixels you want to paint over the telegraph pole. Set your Brush size in the Options bar and you can then brush up against the chimney, safe in the knowledge you won't do any damage.

To remove the telegraph pole seamlessly from this image using Selections you'll need to work around the locomotive chimney with the *Polygonal Lasso* tool. Next, get the inverse of the Selection by going to *Select→ Inverse*.

Now head into the Toolbox and select the *Clone Stamp tool* (S). Hold the *Alt* key to sample the pixels you'd like to use to replace the telegraph pole and brush up against the chimney. Notice how it's not damaged in any way!

MAKE PRECISE SELECTIONS FOR BETTER EDITING

USE THE POLYGONAL LASSO TOOL TO SELECT SUBJECTS, SO YOU CAN MAKE ADJUSTMENTS ACCURATELY

MOST DIGITAL PHOTOS will benefit from improved contrast, but quite often they'll need different adjustments applied to different areas and a global adjustment (one that affects the whole image) just won't cut it. On this picture for instance, we've selectively lightened the climber and darkened the background, to increase the contrast and visual impact. For this of course, we first needed to make a Selection, and as you've already seen, there are plenty of different tools on offer in Photoshop and Elements for this purpose. But because here we need a precise Selection, there's only one tool for the job - the *Polygonal Lasso tool* - and in this tutorial, you'll find out how to use it.

VIDEO LESSON ON THE COVER DISC!

Ps Pse

THE START IMAGE

FILE NAME ***DARTMOOR.JPG***

There's nothing overly wrong with this photograph - it just lacks punch. But by using Selections we can work on separate areas to beef up the contrast and really bring out the best in the photo, adding real visual impact.

USE PRECISE SELECTIONS TO FIX CONTRAST

The *Polygonal Lasso tool* offers masses of versatility because it gives you the ability to make both precise Selections as well as broader more general ones. Its variants, the *Lasso*, which works in a more freehand way, and *Magnetic Lasso*, which automatically follows edges, are quicker, but not accurate enough to pick out a complex subject as we want to here.

Using the *Polygonal Lasso* and clicking on the image, the tool will draw a line between each successive click until you join the last click to the first. Once a shape has been made, the 'marching ants' will appear and, just like any other Selection in Photoshop or Elements, any changes you make to the image will apply only to the area within the Selection.

THE LASSO TOOL OFFERS THE ABILITY TO PERFORM ACCURATE SELECTIONS...

Feathering

Once your precise Selection is made, it will still need feathering so that it'll work with the rest of the picture and create a realistic edge to your adjustments. This is just as important as feathering a broad Selection, but this time we'll use only minimal feathering, as too much softness at the edge will mean a halo is created around the adjustments you're making. On the other hand, if you use no feathering at all, you'll end up with too hard an edge that will look equally unnatural.

Saving Selections

Photoshop and Elements also allow you to save Selections, so if you've spent ages on an intricate piece of work you can save and reload it at any time. Plus, if you save in *.PSD* format, the Selection data will also be saved and you can reload your Selection after closing the image down and re-opening it.

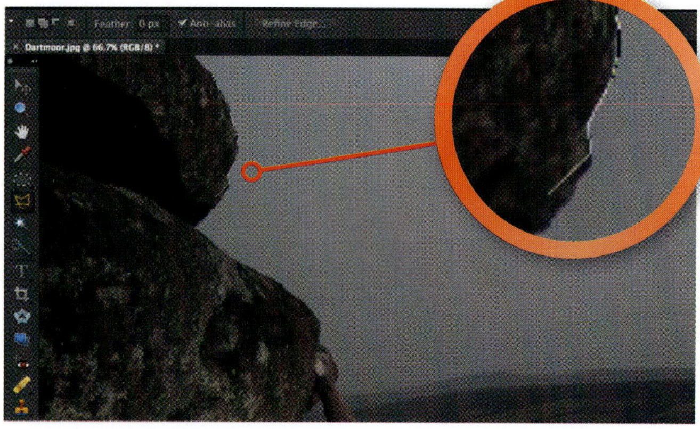

1 START THE SELECTION. Open the image *DARTMOOR.jpg* from the disc then choose the *Polygonal Lasso tool* (shortcut *L*). Start at the top-left of the image and make a Selection around the climber and the foreground rock by clicking along the outline. Double-clicking joins your point back to the start, so make sure you don't click too fast or you may complete the Selection before it's ready.

2 MODIFY THE SELECTION. Click on the *Subtract from Selection* icon (or hold *Alt* as you click) then trace around the edges between the climber's arms and legs. This will deselect the background areas leaving just the subject selected. With your Selection complete go to *Select→ Modify→ Feather* and set the *Radius* to *1 pixel*, then click *OK*.

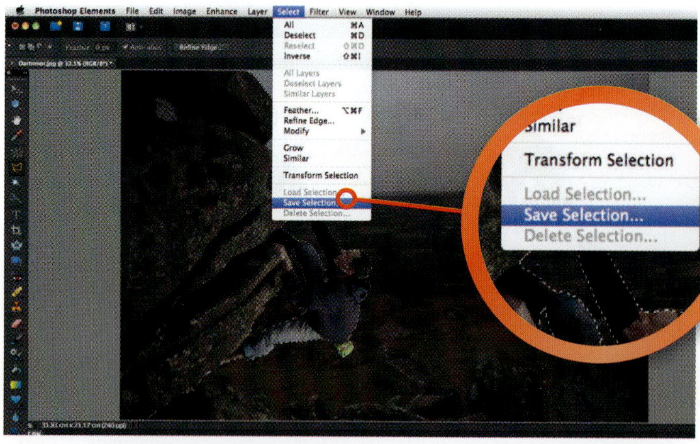

3 SAVE YOUR SELECTION. We'll be needing this Selection again later so it's worth saving it at this point (*Select→ Save Selection*). Set the name to *Climber* - this allows you to reload the Selection again whenever you need it. This selection data is also retained when you save as a *.PSD* file so you can bring up your Selection even after you've closed and re-opened the image.

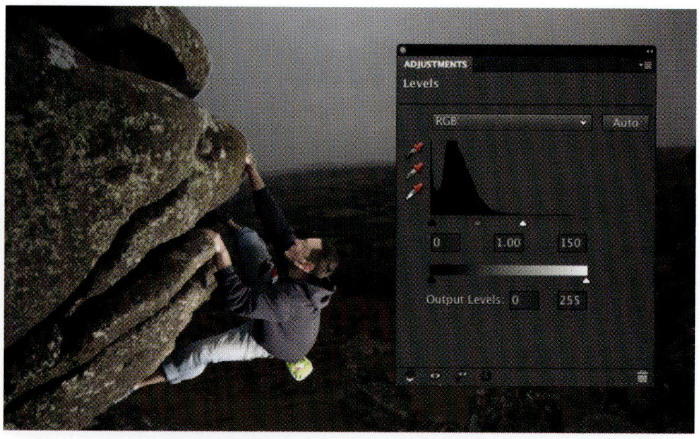

4 LIGHTEN SUBJECT. With your Selection made and saved, it's time to create an Adjustment Layer. Open your *Layers palette* (*Window→ Layers*), click on the *Create a new Adjustment Layer* icon, and then choose *Levels*. In the *Levels palette*, move the White Point slider to the left to about *150* - this should have the effect of lightening the subject nicely. Click *OK* or exit the palette.

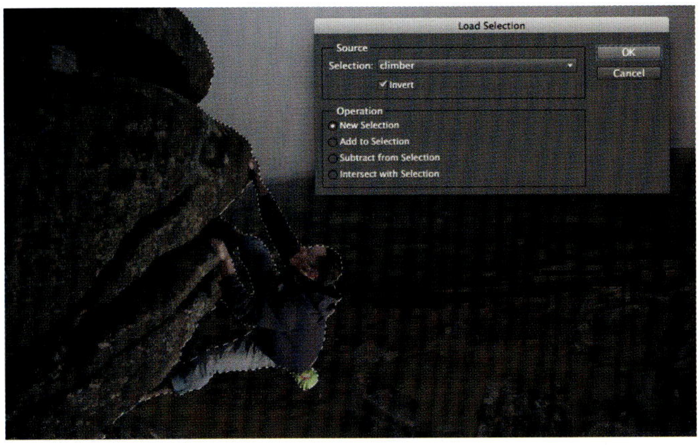

5 **INVERT THE SELECTION.** You'll notice that the Selection has now disappeared, so we need to reload it before we can get the inverse for use on the background. To do this, go to *Select→ Load Selection* and choose *Climber*. To get the inverse of the Selection as you load it, tick the *Inverse* box and hit *OK*. The Selection is now reloaded and inverted, so changes will only apply to the background.

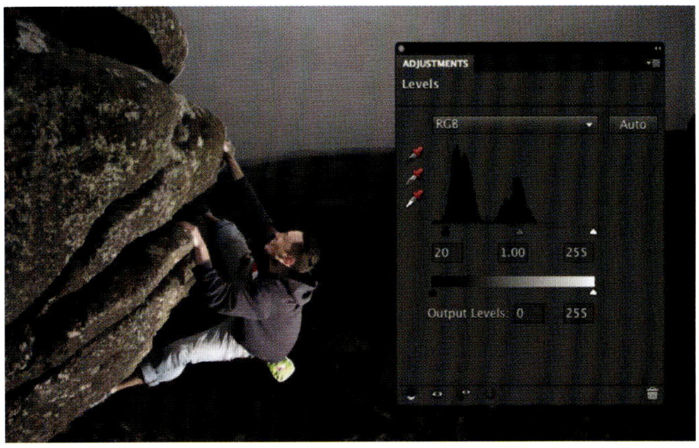

6 **DARKEN THE BACKGROUND.** Again you need to make an Adjustment Layer based on your Selection so, as before, click on the *Create New Adjustment Layer* icon in the *Layers palette* and and choose *Levels*. Now move the Black Point slider up to about *25*. This will darken the background, but of course the climber will be untouched as they're outside the Selection.

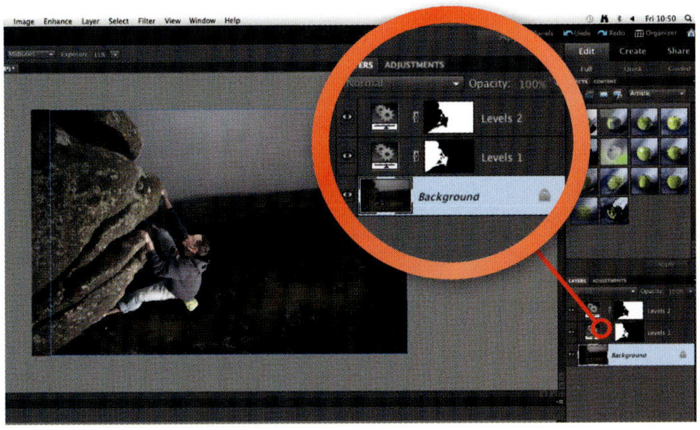

7 **FINE-TUNING.** In your *Layers palette* click on the *Background* Layer and pick the *Dodge tool* from the Toolbox (shortcut *O*). in the Options bar, set the *Exposure* to *15%* and the *Range* to *Midtones*. Now selectively lighten parts of the middle distance, around the rocks and grassy areas, to prevent the background looking too flat.

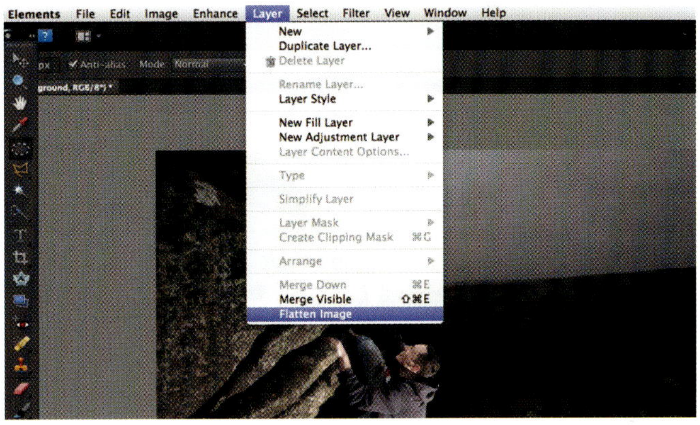

8 **FINISH FLATTEN & SAVE.** Now you're done, it's time to flatten the image. Go to *Layer→ Flatten image* to combine your Layers into one. The last step is to save it - go to *File→ Save as*, and choose *PSD*, so that the Selection made is saved, too, and you can come back and edit it again in the future. Hit *OK* and you're done.

USING PHOTOSHOP'S PEN TOOL

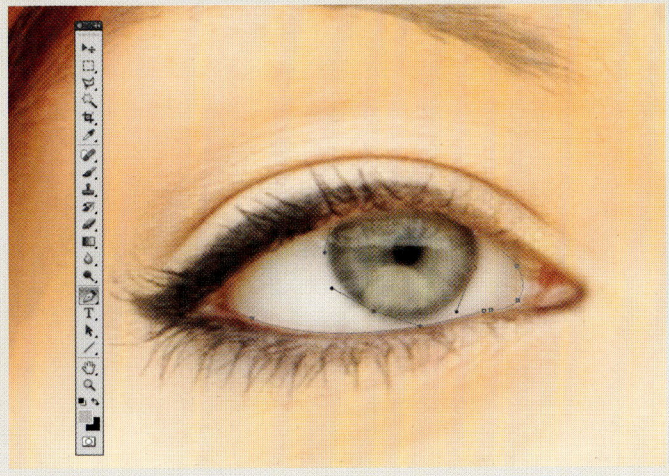

If you have the full version of Photoshop then you'll have access to the *Pen tool*, Photoshop's most precise Selection tool. It works a little differently to the *Lasso tool* in that the *Pen tool* initially creates a *Path*, rather than 'marching ants' and you make this *Path* by laying down Anchor points. Each Anchor point has Control points, and by dragging on these it's possible to bend your Path into curves or sharp corners. This means you can make almost any shape and, unlike the other Selection tools, the *Pen tool* gives a much smoother and more natural-looking edge.

Also, because you're placing Anchor points and creating a Path rather than a regular Selection, any mistakes can be easily rectified by dragging the points around. Once you've drawn back to the starting point it will be complete and can then be turned into a regular Selection. Just go to *Window→ Paths*, right-click on the path and choose *Make Selection*.

CREATE A MULTI-IMAGE MONTAGE

VIDEO LESSON ON THE COVER DISC!

Ps Pse

COMBINE MULTIPLE PHOTOS INTO A SINGLE PIECE OF PHOTO ART USING THE MARQUEE TOOL

A MONTAGE IS AN easy and effective way to present your photos and to make one, all you need is a bunch of snaps - about three or four will do - a copy of either Photoshop or Elements and an understanding of Selections. The *Marquee* tool is the ideal one for the job here, as you'll be able to use it to make large, uniform selections of your photos with just a few clicks.

Once you've made a Selection of the photo to use, you can use the *Refine Edge* option to feather it and help blend it into the montage for a seamless result.

Frame your work

The *Marquee tool* is remarkably versatile and can also be used to make a neat and tidy border for your finished piece, helping to tie all your shots together. A thick, black frame to your montage, as we've used here, will give it a classic look and works well with almost any type of image. You're not restricted to black, though and can choose from the entire colour spectrum - so don't be afraid to get creative and try out some different colours!

Make sure you give this montage technique a try with your own photos, but to practice, the images we've used are included on the disc!

> WHEN IT COMES TO MAKING A MONTAGE, THE MARQUEE TOOL IS THE IDEAL TOOL AS IT'S ABLE TO MAKE LARGE, UNIFORM SELECTIONS

THE START IMAGES

FILE NAMES ***LOLA1.JPG, LOLA2.JPG & LOLA3.JPG***

Although these pics look great by themselves, by merging them to create a montage, we can make a superb piece of photo art. The clutter-free background makes these images ideal candidates for this technique, but with a clever Selection, any shot can be used (see p70).

THE FINAL IMAGE

A montage is a fantastic way to present multiple photos, and takes just minutes to create with the *Marquee tool*.

CORRECTLY SIZING YOUR MONTAGE

Admiring your work on a computer monitor is great, but for pictures this good you're going to want to print your work out. To make life easier when the time comes, it's best to be prepared and make your montage print-ready from the word go.

In this guide, we'll show you how to create your montage on a blank A4-sized canvas, which is ideal for printing on a standard inkjet. If you're looking to create larger or smaller prints, the method is the same, just make your starting canvas to the desired size.

AN A4-SIZED CANVAS IS IDEAL FOR PRINTING WITH A STANDARD HOME INKJET

1 **START CREATE A NEW DOCUMENT.** Load up either Photoshop or Elements and go to *File*→ *New*→ *Blank File* (*File* → *New* for Photoshop users). In the window that appears, change *Preset* to *International Paper*, then, set the *Size* to *A4* (or A3 if you have an A3 printer). Finally, set the *Background Contents* to *White* and click *OK* to create your new blank document.

2 **MAKE A SELECTION.** Go to *File*→ *Open* and open *LOLA1.JPG* from the disc. Now, grab the *Elliptical Marquee* tool (*M*) from the Toolbox and, while holding *Shift*, left-click and drag a large circular Selection around Lola's face – releasing the button when you're done. Adjust the location of the Selection by clicking the left mouse button inside the circle, and dragging it into a new position.

3 **REFINE EDGE.** Click the *Refine Edge* button in the Options bar, or go up to *Select*→ *Refine Edge*. In the dialog box that appears, increase the *Feather* to around *150px* to create a nice soft edge to the Selection. Clicking on the *Preview* options at the bottom will show an on-screen representation of how much your Selection will be feathered. Finally, press *OK* to close the window.

4 **COPY & PASTE.** Press *Ctrl+C* to copy the selected pixels, then switch back to the blank page that you created by going to *Window*→ *Untitled-1*. Press *Ctrl+V* to paste in the pic, then resize it to fit by pressing *Ctrl+T*, making sure *Constrain Proportions* is ticked (Photoshop users, simply hold *Shift*), and pulling on the corner handles. Hit *Enter*, or click the tick when you're finished.

5 **REPEAT THE PROCESS.** Now the first image is in place, we can start to add our other two photos, *LOLA2.JPG* and *LOLA3.JPG* – also located on the cover disc. Simply repeat the same process, starting at Step 2, and if you're using your own snaps, feel free to add as many pictures as you like – although any more than five may start to look a little cluttered.

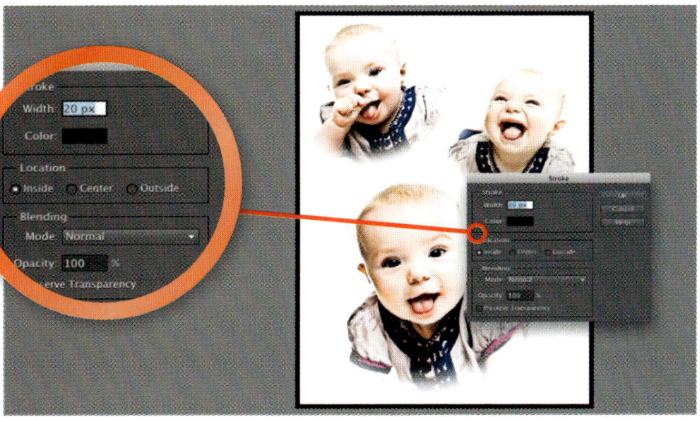

6 ADD A BORDER. With all your pictures in place, create a new Layer by going to *Layer→ New→ Layer*, and press *OK*. Hit *Ctrl+A* to select the entire image, then, go up to *Edit→ Stroke (Outline) Selection* (*Edit→ Stroke* for Photoshop users). Set the *Width* to *20px* and change the *Location* to *Inside*. Finally, adjust the *Color* to a nice solid black (or any other colour of your choice), and press *OK*.

7 FINISH FLATTEN & SAVE. If any of your pictures are being obscured by the newly created border, go to the *Layers palette* (*Window→ Layers*) and highlight the offending Layer by left clicking on it. Next, grab the *Move tool* from the Toolbox and drag the picture to a new position. Once you're happy go to *Layer→ Flatten Image*, and save it as a JPEG, all ready for printing.

USING A SHOT WITH A CLUTTERED BACKGROUND

Using a photo with a cluttered background in your montage may make it look a little busy and distracting. However, with the *Polygonal Lasso tool*, it's possible to remove precise areas from your original circular Selection, leaving only your intended subject behind.

After Step 3 of our step-by-step, simply perform these additional steps...

POLYGONAL LASSO TOOL. Start by selecting the *Polygonal Lasso tool* in the Toolbox, then in the Options bar, set *Feather* to *1px*. Zoom in closer to your photo by pressing *Ctrl* and + a few times to get a good close-up view of the picture.

SUBTRACT FROM YOUR SELECTION. In the Options bar, click on *Subtract from Selection*, then left-click where you'd like to start removing from the Selection. In this case we've carefully clicked around the edge of the subject until we reached the other side. Once you're on the other side, left-click to the edge of your canvas and start to select around the outside of your image until you're back to the starting point (as shown).

REMOVE ANY OTHER AREAS. Continue to remove any other unwanted areas of your Selection by repeating the previous step (the area under the groom's arm here). Once you've done this you'll have a Selection that mixes a broad, soft feather around the outside, with a more precise cut-out of the subject. Now continue the montage guide from Step 4.

CHAPTER 4
USING RAW

EDIT YOUR CAMERA'S RAW FILES FOR TOP QUALITY RESULTS

Remember, when you see this icon, there's a video lesson of the technique on the cover DVD.

P90 MAKE BRILLIANT MONO PICS

Use the Basic tab in Photoshop or Elements' Camera Raw interface to create dramatic black & white pictures that are bursting with undiscovered detail.

P94 TACKLE TRICKY EXPOSURES

RAW offers great control over the exposure in your pics and by combining two separate RAW conversions you'll get perfect lighting.

LEARN WITH US!

IF YOU WANT THE ULTIMATE IN IMAGE QUALITY, YOU NEED TO BE USING RAW. FORTUNATELY IT'S EASY TO DO AND IN THIS CHAPTER YOU'LL FIND OUT HOW...

P86 MAKE A BASIC RAW CONVERSION TO IMPROVE DRAB & DULL IMAGES

Using RAW it's easy to improve highlight and shadow detail, get brighter colours and enhance the sharpness of your pictures.

P98 GET CREATIVE WITH RAW FILES AND APPLY A VINTAGE PHOTO EFFECT

There's so much more to RAW than simply controlling exposure - you can apply fun creative effects to your pictures, too. Check out this technique and see how to give a picture the antique look.

P102 ADVANCED SKILLS IN RAW

If you want the ultimate in control you need to start using Camera Raw's Local Adjustment tools, which let you edit individual parts of your picture - it's the smart way to work!

RAW LETS YOU MAKE CHANGES TO AN IMAGE THAT WOULD BE IMPOSSIBLE WITH A JPEG!

MANY PEOPLE THINK THAT using RAW gives you improved image quality and while this is true, the form it comes in can be a little confusing. Shooting in RAW doesn't give you more pixels to play with or extra sharpness in your pictures, it's actually much more about flexibility and the ability to control results.

All pictures start out as RAW data, but most of the time this is compressed into a JPEG before it's output. In this compression, some of the data is discarded and it's then fixed, but when you open a RAW file into Photoshop, all the original pure data is still there for you to use, meaning you can make a host of changes to your picture that wouldn't be as successful with a JPEG.

Say, for instance, one part of the picture is too bright, like the sky. In a JPEG, nothing can be done because the detail has been lost, but in a RAW file it can be brought back using the Exposure slider. The same applies to returning shadow details, increasing the intensity of colour and controlling a picture's white balance for more accurate hues.

But it doesn't end there, you can apply creative effects by the dozen, too. Just turn the page to start learning.

VIDEO LESSON ON THE COVER DISC!

Ps Pse

When you see this logo, it means there's an in-depth video lesson on our cover disc that accompanies the technique. Watch and learn as one of our experts takes you through the project, step by step!

GET STARTED WITH RAW

THE CAMERA RAW CONVERTER IS YOUR PATH TO BETTER IMAGES – AND YOU CAN FIND OUT WHAT MAKES IT TICK RIGHT HERE...

Once you open a RAW into Photoshop or Elements the Adobe Camera Raw interface will launch and, while to newcomers it may seem complicated, it's really just like an oversized Photoshop palette. Many of the tools involved will also be familiar to Photoshop or Elements users, so you'll soon feel right at home with the interface and ready to get working.

The tools you need

Over the next few pages we'll take a look at the most useful tools and controls in the Camera Raw interface and tell you what they do when applied to your pics. We'll then make a basic RAW conversion from an image on the disc. The screen on the right is from Elements 9, so you may spot some differences if you're running an older copy of Elements or a version of its big brother, the Photoshop CS series. Differences will be minor, though, because here we're looking at the basic tools. Take a quick look around to familiarise yourself with them, then turn over to start using them in action - it's easier than you think!

HELP & SAVE
The HELP button launches the Adobe Community Help page, while SAVE IMAGE... lets you save the converted RAW file without opening it. This is really useful when making batch conversions - converting multiple RAWs using the same settings.

DEPTH
This lets you set the resulting bit-depth of your converted file for increased quality, though it's best left on 8-bits per channel unless you really want or need 16-bit images (many functions in Photoshop can't be used on them).

THE TOOLBAR
You'll recognise many of these tools from the main image-editing area of Photoshop or Elements, and they're mainly used to navigate around the image, crop, straighten or rotate it.

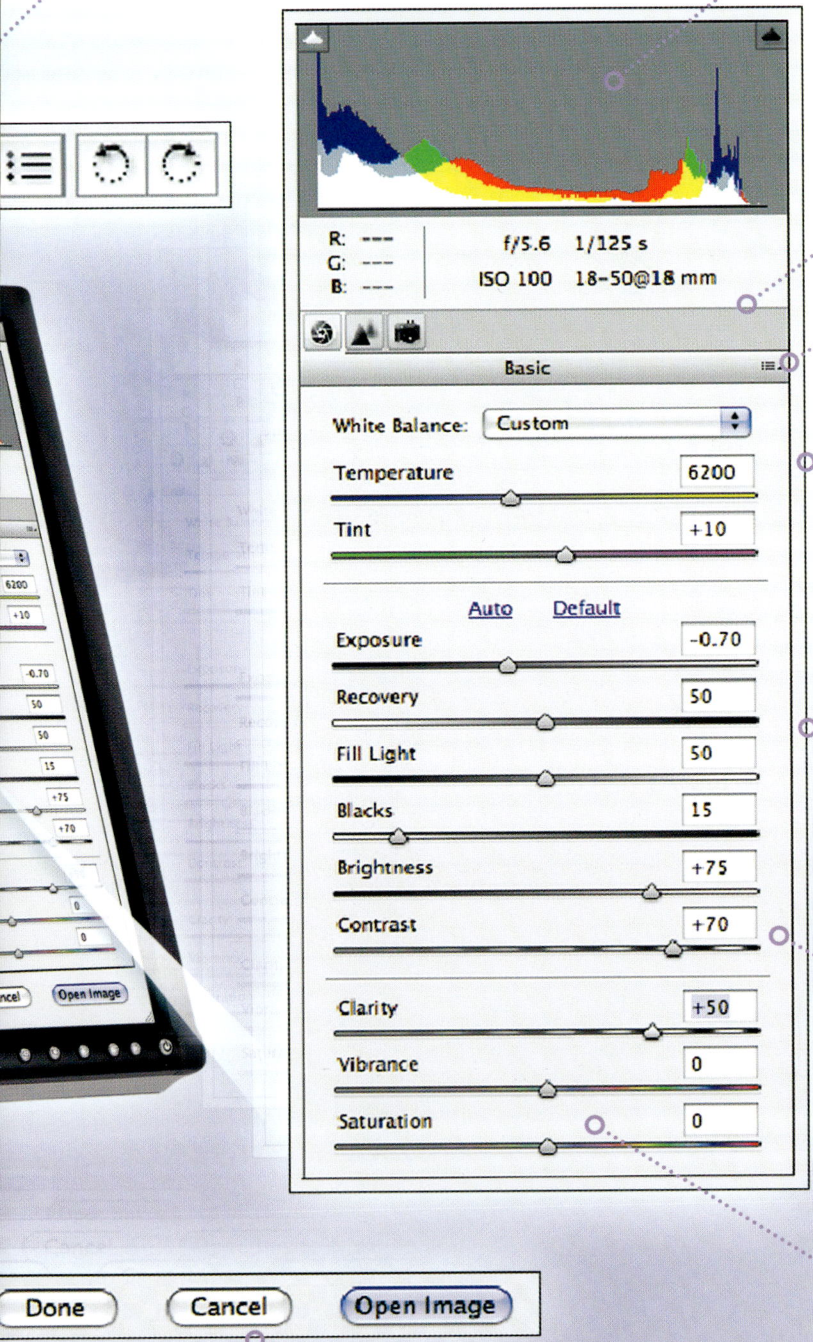

IMAGE HISTOGRAM
This chart shows how the tonal values are distributed throughout the image you're working on and responds to changes you make using the sliders below. The luminance value runs from left to right, so you can tell if a picture is heavy on the shadows (chart to the left) or the highlights (to the right). You can also activate the SHADOWS & HIGHLIGHTS CLIPPING WARNINGS here, which overlay a warning on the image - areas of red showing where highlights are clipped into pure white and have lost detail, and blue meaning detail has been lost in shadow.

FILE INFO & TABS
Under the Histogram you'll find info about how your photo was shot and below that are the Tabs, in this version: *Basic* (which is currently open), *Detail* and *Camera Calibration*.

FLY-OUT MENU
Here you'll find options to reset the Camera Raw Defaults, taking you back to an unedited starting point.

WHITE BALANCE & TEMPERATURE
The drop-down WHITE BALANCE list has preset options (*Tungsten, Daylight, Cloudy* etc) like those on your camera. These can be fine-tuned by the TEMPERATURE slider letting you warm up or cool down colours in relation to the ambient light in which it was shot. The TINT slider compensates for any green or magenta colour cast.

EXPOSURE, RECOVERY, FILL LIGHT & BLACKS
The EXPOSURE slider adjusts overall image brightness, and is biased towards the highlights. Decreasing it will darken your pic and increasing it will make it brighter. RECOVERY is used to restore detail in highlight areas and FILL LIGHT recovers detail from the shadow areas, but avoids brightening the very deepest blacks. Finally BLACKS lets you darken (or lighten) the very lowest part of the tonal range; the shadows of the image.

BRIGHTNESS, CONTRAST & CLARITY
The BRIGHTNESS slider lightens or darkens all of the tones in your image within the set black and white points, while CONTRAST makes the mid-to-light tones brighter and the mid-to-dark tones darker, creating separation and depth. The CLARITY slider adds definition by increasing the contrast around edges within your photo, but can cause haloes if it's used too aggressively.

VIBRANCE & SATURATION
VIBRANCE adjusts the intensity of the least-saturated colours in the picture and has less effect on the more-saturated ones, which helps you avoid blocking out colours, while SATURATION controls all the colours equally, so should be used sparingly.

DONE, CANCEL & OPEN IMAGE
The final buttons you'll use in the Camera Raw interface. DONE closes the image while retaining any settings you've changed. CANCEL closes the image *without* recording changes and OPEN IMAGE will take the picture in the full image-editing area of Photoshop or Elements for further work.

TURN OVER TO SEE CAMERA RAW IN ACTION

HOW TO MAKE A BASIC RAW CONVERSION

Now we've taken a look at the Camera Raw interface it's time to get stuck into a proper RAW conversion. We'll be using the file called *WELLS.dng* from the cover disc, so just load it up (or one of your own RAWs) and give it a try. By following this guide you'll learn all about the tools you really need, and discover that RAW is the way to go if you want great pictures.

The pic we'll be using has various problems, all of which are common to many landscape shots and other images. For instance its colours are a little too cold, so it could do with warming up, and this is easy to achieve using the White Balance tool, menu or Temperature slider. But the biggest problem – and by association the greatest benefit of using RAW – is that we need to correct the exposure. Shot towards the sun, the sky is much too bright, and you can plainly see this as soon as you open the file by clicking on the Highlight clipping warning button.

Any areas which are pure white will carry a red overlay and you'll clearly be able to see that the top left of the picture is very burnt out with no cloud detail remaining.

THE START IMAGE

FILENAME
WELLS.DNG
The pic used in this technique is included on the cover disc, so use it for practice and then try it out on your own images.

With a JPEG, nothing could be done – the detail would have been lost for good, but in a RAW file it can be brought back using the Exposure and Recovery sliders. Remember, though, that there's no 'correct' recipe for a RAW conversion – but get used to what the sliders do and you'll be well equipped to make your own.

1 OPEN & CROP THE IMAGE. In Photoshop or Elements, go to *File→ Open* and choose the picture called *WELLS.dng*. Click *Open* and the Camera Raw interface will launch. Now click on the *Straighten tool* and drag it out along the horizon to match the angle. Release the button and you'll see a crop box appear, angled to correct any slant in your image. Drag the corner handles in a little, then hit *Return*.

2 CORRECT THE COLOURS. As mentioned above, the picture could do with warming up. To do it, either pick the *White Balance* tool from the toolbar and click on a neutral grey tone in the image (like the grey clouds), or for a more manual control, take the *Temperature* slider and move it up or down. To make the most of the colours in our picture, we set it to *6200* with the *Tint* at *+10*.

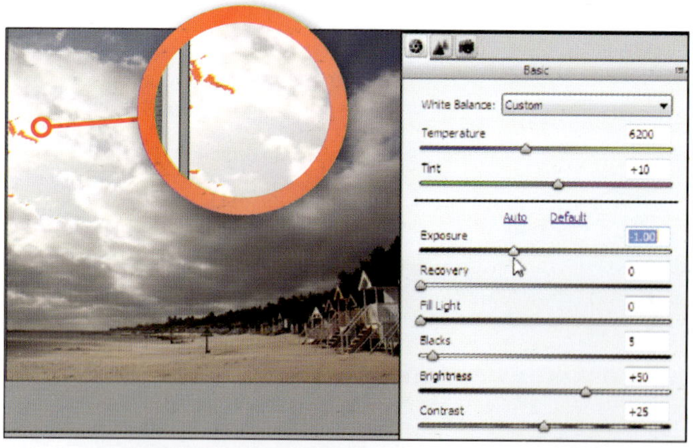

3 CONTROL THE HIGHLIGHTS. Switch on the Highlight clipping warnings next to the Histogram and you'll see lots of red in the sky showing it's burnt out. Now set the *Exposure* to *-1.00* and the *Recovery* slider to *15* and most of, if not all the red warnings will disappear. If you're not keen on the clipping warnings covering your pic, you can instead hold *Alt* as you move the slider to toggle a similar effect.

4 IMPROVE THE SHADOW AREAS. By moving the *Exposure* slider to a negative value we've darkened the sky but also the rest of the scene. To bring it back, move the *Fill Light* slider to *70*, which will lighten these shadow areas, but leave them looking a little washed out. To address this, move the *Blacks* to *30*, using the *Alt*-key preview to make sure they aren't too heavy in your shot.

5 **ADD SOME CONTRAST.** As the pic was shot into the sun, the overall contrast has taken a bit of a hit, so for a bit more punch move the *Contrast* slider to about *+70*. We can also lighten up the picture a little using the *Brightness* slider and setting it *+60*. Next move the *Clarity* to about *+50*, which will add some definition to the beach huts making the picture look more detailed.

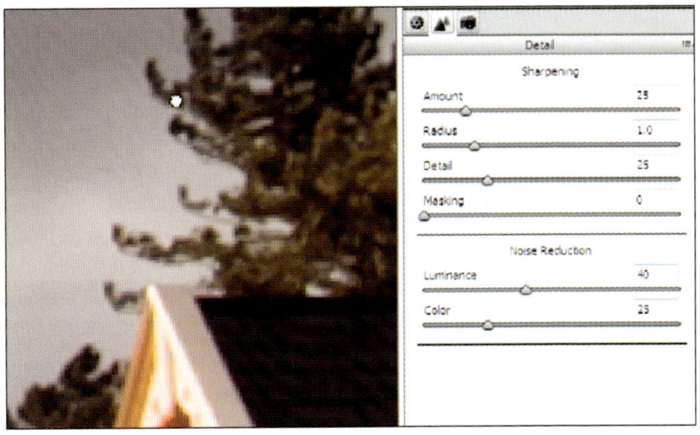

6 **WORK UP THE COLOURS.** There are some lovely brightly-coloured beach huts in the picture, but at present their colours are a little muted. We can correct this with the *Vibrance* and *Saturation* sliders. The *Vibrance* slider works on the least-saturated colours, so first move this up to *+20* to even things out, then use *+20* for *Saturation*, too, making the picture more colourful overall.

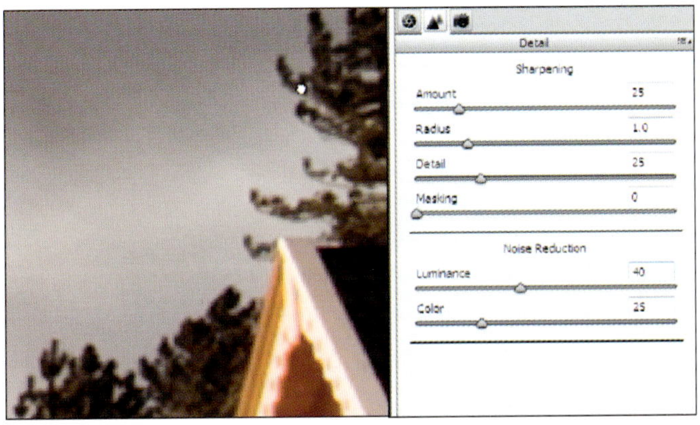

7 **SOFTEN THE NOISE.** Click on the *Detail* tab and move down to the *Noise Reduction* sliders. Before using them, zoom in to a *100%* view, so you can see the changes taking place. Now keep your eye on the sky as you move the *Luminance* slider to around *40* and you'll see the graininess much reduced. Move the *Color* slider up until any red, green or blue specs disappear - *25* works on our picture here.

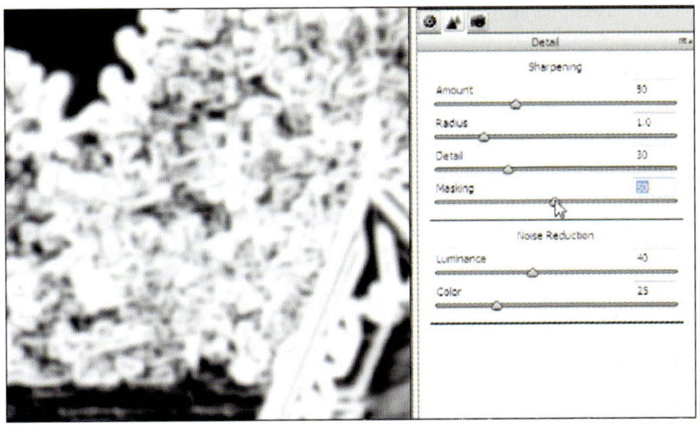

8 FINISH **SHARPEN THE PIC.** We can also improve sharpness in RAW. First move the *Amount* (which controls the overall level of sharpening) to around *50*, and the *Radius* (which governs how broad the effect is) to *1.0*. Next, set the *Detail* to *30*, which will keep the sharpening around edges within your pic and the *Masking* to *50*, so smooth areas like the sky are omitted. Now click *Open Image*. That's it!

HOW TO CONVERT MULTIPLE RAWS AT THE SAME TIME

There's a lot of fine control which goes into a RAW conversion and to the uninitiated it can seem like too much effort, especially when you need to convert multiple shots. The benefit is plain though and if you're serious about achieving the very best images, RAW is something that just can't be beaten. There are some ways to save time however, and one of them is to convert lots of RAWs at the same time.

So long as your subject matter is pretty similar from one shot to the next - lots of pictures of the same landscape scene or multiple studio portraits for instance - you can load multiple RAWs into the converter and apply the same settings to all of them. To do it, go to *File → Open* and highlight all of the RAWs you want to convert. Click *Open* and once they appear in the RAW converter, click the *Select All* button. Now make your changes and they'll be applied to all of the RAWs you've loaded at once. Easy!

THE FINAL IMAGE
By using the Adobe Camera Raw converter to turn our original colour image to black & white we've been able to create this superb mono image, which is bursting with detail.

CREATE SUPERB MONO IMAGES FROM RAW

MAKE BLACK & WHITE IMAGES WITH BAGS OF GRITTY DETAIL AND DRAMATIC CONTRAST - IT'S EASY WHEN YOU GO MONO IN RAW

VIDEO LESSON ON THE COVER DISC!

Ps Pse

WORKING IN BLACK & WHITE is perhaps the quickest and most dramatic way that you can improve your images. It's a style in which its easy to create striking shots, because without colour, an image is reduced to the more simple elements of form, texture and contrast.

Working in RAW is the best way to go mono because you can use the sliders within the Adobe Camera Raw converter to control exposure to make sure you have the maximum amount of detail in your picture. And free from the constraints of colour, you can also apply more aggressive adjustments without so much fear of the image breaking up and looking unsightly. Still not convinced? Give this technique a try and you'll definitely believe us!

THE START IMAGE

FILE NAME *SEAVIXEN.DNG*
Despite being sharply focused, the start image is lacking drama - something we can quickly introduce during our RAW conversion. By doing it using our special RAW-to-mono recipe you'll create an image that's full of detail and shows off the subject at its absolute best.

HOW RAW MAKES GREAT MONO EASY...

In this Photoshop and Elements technique you'll learn how to take one of your full-colour RAW files and turn it into a stunning black & white image. Sounds simple, right? Well yes and no. Once you follow the technique you'll find it's easy to do, but if you think creating great monotone images from RAW is just a matter of dragging the Saturation slider to -100, you're in for a real treat because we'll be doing a little more creative tinkering than that.

There are so many ways you can convert to black & white in Photoshop that you might also be wondering why you'd want to do it from RAW in the first place – the answer is quality. By going mono directly from a RAW you can push your conversion amazingly hard, much more so than with a JPEG, and with the colour removed from your image you're free to wring every last drop of drama and detail out of the image without worrying about unsightly shifts in hue or fringeing.

So what do we mean by pushing the conversion hard? It's all about grabbing the sliders and pushing them to their extremes, so while you might normally shy away from using large amounts of Fill Light or from using very high or low-settings on the Temperature slider, these are the choices that make this technique work. With this kind of aggressive RAW conversion you may find that an increase in Noise can be a by-product, but the extra grain is so suited to mono images that it almost becomes a positive addition to the style of your shot.

All the tools we'll be using are available in the Basic tab, so you can do it in any version of Adobe Camera Raw. And once you've seen how much better the results can be than from a simple desaturated RAW file, you'll never look back.

> YOU'LL BE FREE TO WRING EVERY LAST DROP OF DRAMA FROM YOUR IMAGE...

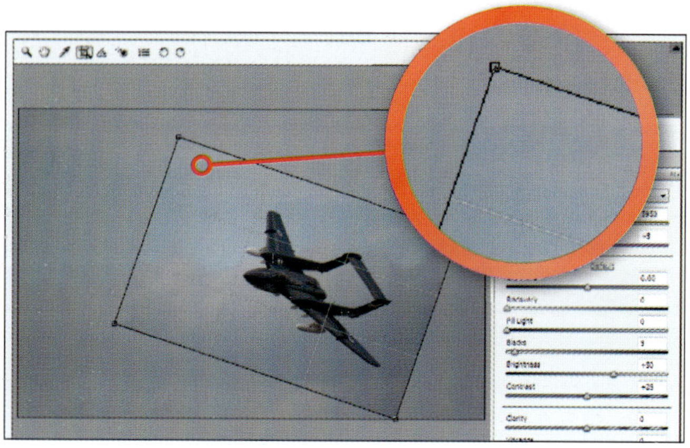

1 START **OPEN AND CROP.** Open the picture called *SEAVIXEN.dng* from the cover disc and once the Adobe Camera Raw interface has launched click on the *Crop tool* from the top of the palette. Drag it out over the subject, losing a little of the dead space and then moving your cursor outside the crop box, click and drag to rotate it clockwise as shown above. Hit *Return* when you're done.

2 **DESATURATE THE IMAGE.** Now, to take all of the colour out of the picture, move down to the bottom of the palette and click and drag the *Saturation* slider all the way to *-100*. The *Vibrance* slider can be left at *0*, because when moved to *-100*, there's no colour left in the image for it to control. You'll now have a black & white picture, but it'll look a bit grey and washed out.

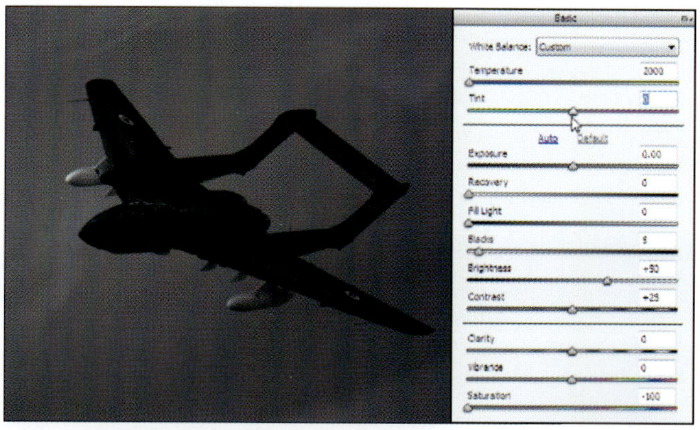

3 **SET THE TEMPERATURE & TINT.** Although all of the colour has gone, the *Temperature* slider which controls White Balance can still have a big effect. Move it to the extremes of the scale and you'll see your picture take on some interesting effects. Here we've set it to a value of *2000* which darkens the sky. The *Tint* slider can work in a similar way, though we left ours at around *0*.

4 **CONTROL THE EXPOSURE.** The picture will be looking a little dark at this point, so click and drag the Exposure slider to a setting of *+2.50*. This will vary if you're using your own image, but just hold the *Alt* key as you move the slider and stop when white areas start growing too large in the clipping preview. Moving the *Recovery* slider will minimise clipped highlights and here it's set to *30*.

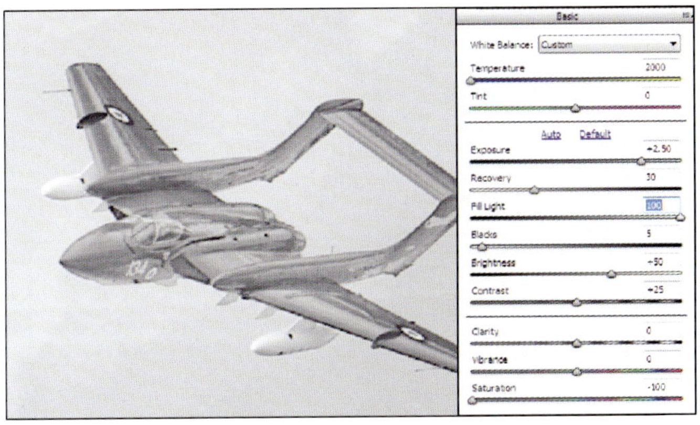

5 **ENHANCE THE SHADOW AREAS.** Now move down to the *Fill Light* slider and drag it all the way to *100*. You'll notice lots of detail appear as the shadow areas of the picture are lightened. We've used the maximum amount available on our example image, but you should experiment to see what works best on your own shots, and stop when the level of detail looks right.

6 **ADD DEPTH TO THE SHADOWS.** Using a very high setting for *Fill Light* will make the picture look a little washed out, but you can anchor the shadows once more using the *Blacks* slider. As you did with the Exposure and Highlight sliders, hold the *Alt* key while dragging the *Blacks* slider and a clipping preview will show when solid areas of black are appearing – we stopped at a setting of *25*.

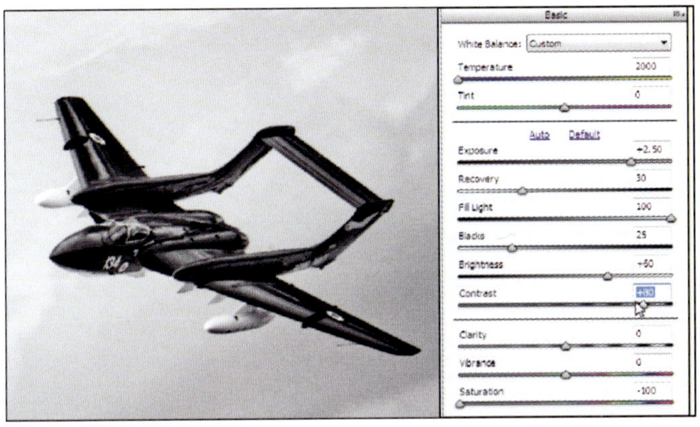

7 **INCREASE CONTRAST.** You'll now have a good balance, with 'true' highlight and shadow areas on show. The next step is to increase the *Contrast*, so drag that slider to the right to push more of the midtones into the highlight and shadow areas. We settled on around 80, but try higher settings to see what looks right on your image. We also lightened the pic a little, moving *Brightness* to *+60*.

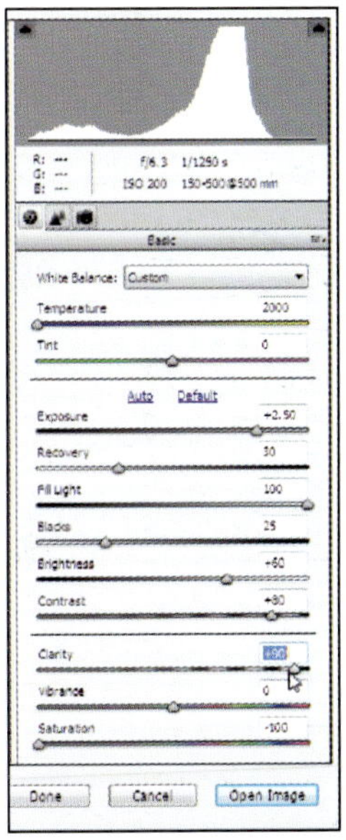

8 **FINISH CRISP UP THE DETAILS.** Now move the *Clarity* slider up to a high setting, giving the picture more definition. Again, this is something you can do more freely in mono, so take it as high as you like – we chose a setting of *+90*. Finally click on the *Detail* tab and, under *Noise Reduction* set *Luminance* to *+80*, then click *Open image* and you're done!

GET EVEN BETTER MONO USING RAW'S HSL/GRAYSCALE TAB

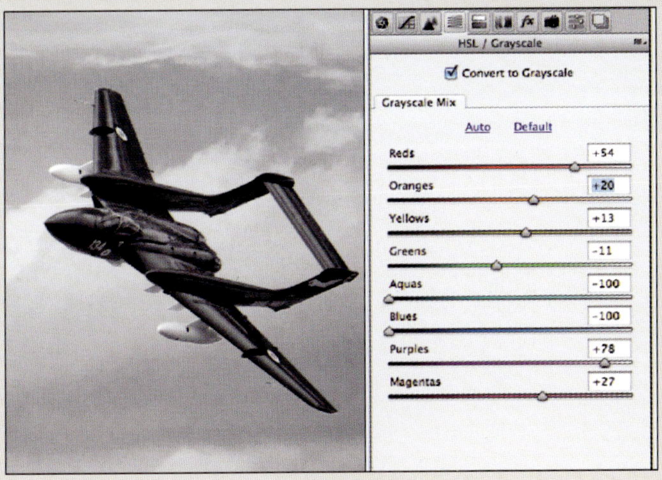

If you have the full version of Photoshop you can take even more control of your black & white images using the HSL/Grayscale tab within Adobe Camera Raw. This controls the Hue, Saturation and Lightness of the individual colours in your image, but much like using the Temperature slider in the technique above, just because your picture is desaturated doesn't mean you can't still use this tab. All the colour information is still in the file for you to play with.

To give it a go, open the image as normal and then, instead of following the steps above click on the HSL/Grayscale tab (the fourth one along. Next click the Convert to Grayscale option and you'll be presented with sliders under the Grayscale mix heading. Now simply move these around until you get a good blend. Lower values will darken those previously coloured parts of the image they correspond to, and high ones will lighten them. Give it a go for a really creative look.

BALANCE YOUR SHOTS IN RAW

PERFECT YOUR PICTURES BY BLENDING TOGETHER DIFFERENT RAW CONVERSIONS OF THE SAME IMAGE

VIDEO LESSON ON THE COVER DISC!

Ps Pse

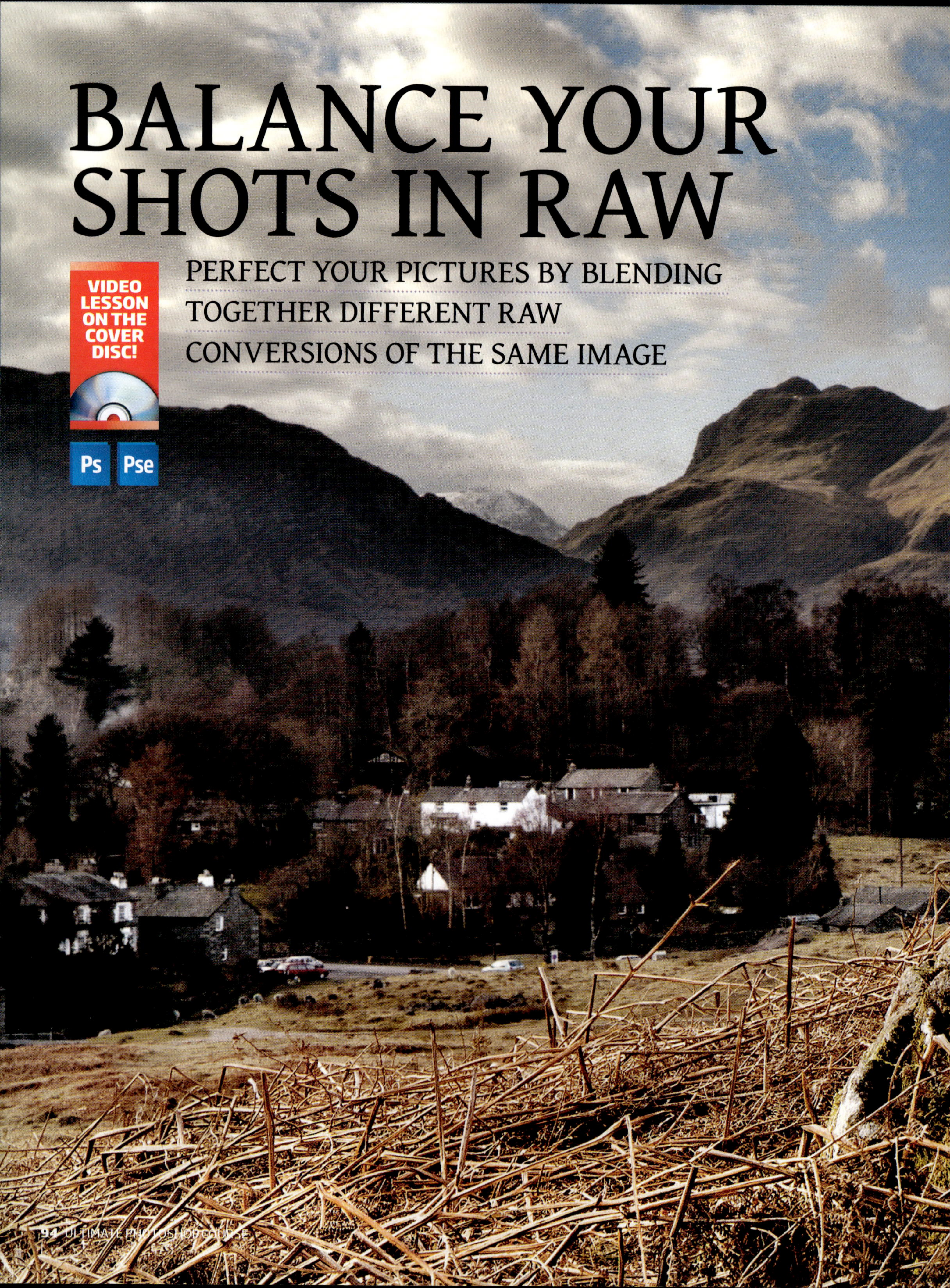

ONE OF THE BIGGEST challenges for a landscape photographer is overcoming contrast. All too often, the sky is much brighter than the foreground, and because your camera can't take in the same range of brightness as your eyes, it means your shots will look unbalanced. If you expose correctly for the sky, your land will be too dark for a pleasing image, and if you allow the foreground to govern your exposure settings, the sky will be burnt out into a empty white patch that's devoid of detail. A solution can be found by using graduated Neutral Density filters over the lens to darken the sky, but this can be fiddly and time consuming. Want a better fix for an age-old problem? Of course you do – just read on to find it...

THE START IMAGE

FILENAME
LANGDALE.DNG
The pic used in this technique is included on the cover disc, so have a practise and then try it out on your own images.

THE FINAL IMAGE
Our sky and foreground are nicely balanced, with good levels of detail in both. It's a world apart from our starting point.

1 START **ASSESS THE PROBLEM.** Open *LANGDALE.dng* into Photoshop or Elements and it'll load into Adobe Camera Raw. You'll see a very common landscape problem - the foreground is very under-exposed compared to the sky. To solve this we'll make two conversions - one for the sky and one for the land - and then we'll blend them together. They're from the same file so they'll line up perfectly.

2 **MAKE THE SKY CONVERSION.** Ignoring the dark foreground and focusing solely on the sky, tweak the sliders in the RAW converter to get the best-looking result. The settings you use will be different for each image you convert, but for our file we went for *Temperature 6300, Tint +10, Exposure -0.20, Brightness +50* and *Contrast +18*. All the other settings were on zero.

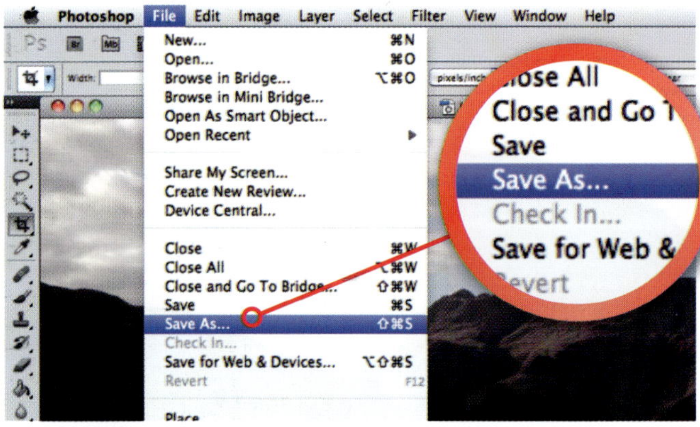

3 **OPEN AND SAVE THE SKY.** Click on *Open Image* at the bottom of the RAW dialog, and the picture will load into the regular interface. It's a good idea to save this conversion so you can always come back to it, so go to *File➔Save As* and call the image *Langdale Sky*. Photoshop's native format will give the best quality, so pick that in *Save As*. Once you've done this, just leave it on screen.

4 **MAKE THE LAND CONVERSION.** Open the *LANGDALE.dng* file again, and you'll bring up the RAW with the settings you've just made. Now ignore the sky and adjust the sliders to give a good-looking foreground. On our image, we went for *Temperature 6450, Tint +10, Exposure +1.90, Fill Light 21, Blacks 16, Brightness +50* and *Contrast +40*. All other settings were on zero. Click *Open Image* again.

5 **COMBINE THE TWO VERSIONS.** Once the foreground conversion appears, hit *Ctrl+A* to select it, and then *Ctrl+C* to copy it. You can now close it by hitting *Ctrl+W* (you don't need to save it). The image with the good sky will now be on screen, so hit *Ctrl+V* and your foreground conversion will be pasted into the same document. Go to *Window➔Layers* and you'll see them stacked in the *Layers palette*.

6 **BLEND THE PICS TOGETHER.** To get the best from both conversions, pick up the *Eraser tool* and in the Options bar at the top of the screen, choose a large, soft-edged brush, and run it across the sky to reveal the better sky from the Layer beneath. As you approach the skyline, drop the *Opacity* to around *50%*, and work over the mountains to get a natural-looking blend between the two Layers.

7 ADD A LITTLE DRAMA. We're getting close now, but the sky could do with a bit of extra oomph. With the *Lasso tool*, select the top part of the sky and then click the *Refine Edge* button and move the *Feather* slider to *150px*. In the *Layers palette*, click the *Adjustment Layer* icon and choose *Levels* from the list, then move the black point and mid point sliders a little to the right to darken the sky.

8 FINISH WARM UP THE IMAGE. Click the *Adjustment Layer* icon once more and again, select *Levels*. In the *Levels palette*, click where it says *RGB* and choose the *Red* channel. Move the midpoint slider a little to the left. Now click where it says *Red* and choose the *Blue* channel. Move the same slider slightly to the right, and you'll have a fabulous warm-up effect to finish off your picture.

USING LAYER MASKS TO BLEND YOUR DIFFERENT RAW CONVERSIONS

In this exercise, we've used the *Eraser tool* to create the blend between one RAW conversion and the other. While this is intuitive, it's not the most refined way of working, as once you've removed the pixels you have no simple way of backtracking other than the *Undo History* - and this isn't retained when you save the file. A better, more advanced method is to use a Layer Mask instead, as this lets you hide or reveal the pixels from the Layer beneath, without removing them. All versions of Photoshop feature Layer Masks, and Elements 9 and 10 also have them, too. Instead of using the Eraser on Step 6, click the *Layer Mask* icon in the Layers palette. Then you simply use a black paintbrush to 'make a hole' in the Layer and reveal the pixels from beneath, or use a white brush to hide them.

USE RAW FOR EASY RETRO FILM EFFECTS

VIDEO LESSON ON THE COVER DISC!

Ps Pse

ADD TONING AND COLOUR EFFECTS TO YOUR RAW FILES FOR A BRILLIANT VINTAGE LOOK

THE START IMAGE

FILE NAMES HOMEGUARD.DNG
The start image used in this technique and the accompanying video lesson can be found in the *Start Images* folder on the cover disc. Just copy it to your PC and run through the lesson, then have a go with your own images.

THE FINAL IMAGE
With suitable toning and faded colours, this modern RAW file becomes a dead ringer for an aged, distressed vintage print.

COOK UP A RETRO FILM EFFECT IN RAW…

Throughout this chapter we've been looking at how editing your camera's RAW files can help you get better pictures, but RAW isn't just about improving image quality - you can use it to apply great creative effects, too! That's what we'll be doing in this technique, taking a regular looking image and giving it a vintage make-over, using some of the lesser-used tabs within the Adobe Camera Raw interface. In a few clicks you'll discover that you can give any picture a faded and vintage charm.

We'll first be using the *HSL / Grayscale* tab to change the colours in the picture, making them somewhat less than true to life and mimicking the hit-and-miss results of early colour film and the look of a decaying print. Next we'll use the *Split Toning* tab to apply separate hues to the highlights and shadows of our picture, furthering the vintage effect, before finally using the *FX* tab to place a light vignette on the image and also give it a light dusting of film grain.

Now if you're looking at your version of Adobe Camera Raw and you can't find those tabs, you're almost certainly running Photoshop Elements, or an older version of Photoshop CS - something before Photoshop CS3 - because these tabs only appear in the later versions. It's just one of the extras that come with the full package.

Before adding the vintage effect we will need to apply a few basic exposure changes under the Basic tab to make sure there's plenty of detail in the image.

The picture, *HOMEGUARD.dng* is on the CD for you to practice with, but if you want to try it out on your own shots, remember you're not limited to retro-styled subjects - it can give a nice feel to contemporary portraits, too.

WE'LL USE VARIOUS TABS IN RAW TO GIVE OUR PICTURE A FADED VINTAGE CHARM…

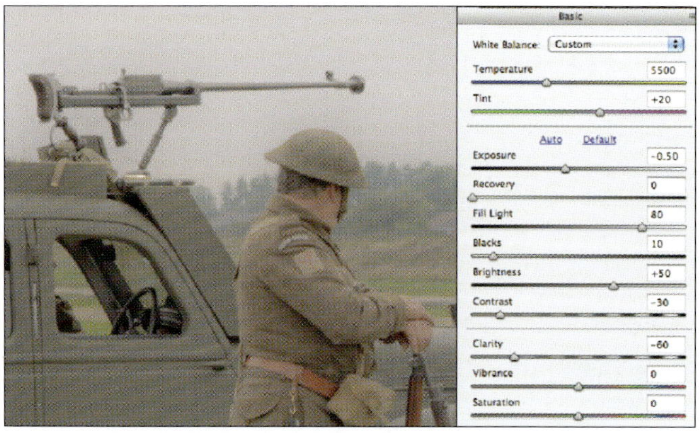

1 START **OPEN & USE THE BASIC TAB.** Open the image called *HOMEGUARD.dng* from the disc to launch the Camera Raw Converter, then set the White Balance to *Daylight*, Tint to *+20*, Exposure to *-0.50*, Recovery to *0*, Fill Light to *80*, Blacks to *10*, Brightness to *+50*, Contrast to *-30* and Clarity to *-60* (the latter two to give the pic a faded look). Finally leave Saturation and Vibrance sliders at *0*.

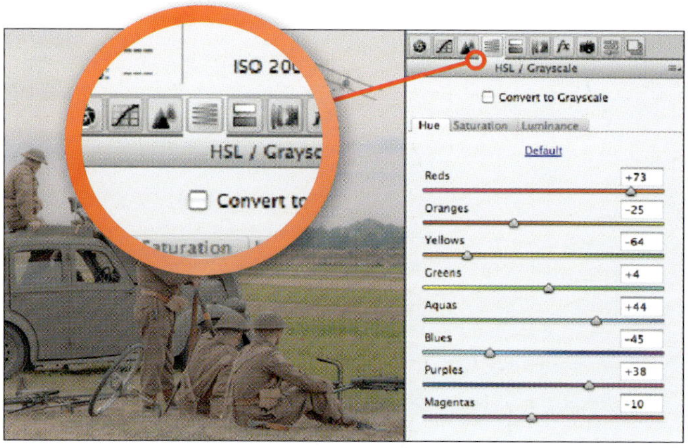

2 **CHANGE THE COLOUR RANGE.** Now, click on the *HSL / Grayscale* tab (the fourth one along in the full version of Photoshop). Here you can control the individual colours that make up the image, independently altering their Hue, Saturation and Luminance to suit. Start by making the colours less true to life under the Hue tab by setting the sliders as shown above.

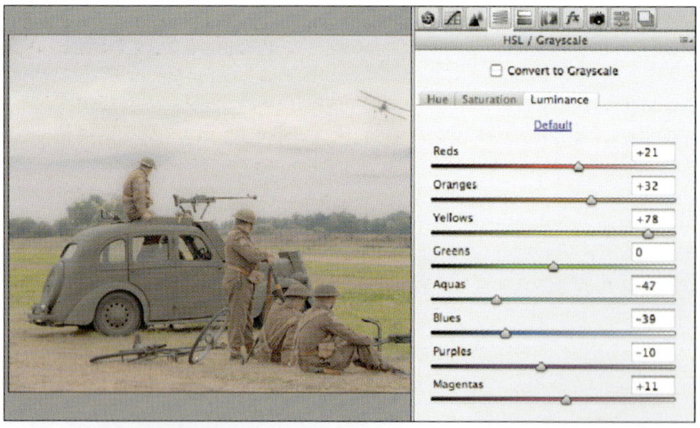

3 **ALTER LUMINANCE.** Next click on the *Luminance* settings. Here you can control the brightness of individual colours, so for instance if you want to make the green grass in a picture lighter, but not alter anything else, you'd move the *Greens* and *Yellows* sliders up. Again, for our example pic, follow the settings above, but when using your own shots make sure you experiment to see what looks best.

4 **CONTROL SATURATION.** Finally, under the HSL / Grayscale tab, click on the *Saturation* settings. These control the intensity of individual colours, and in the case of our example image, we want to increase saturation in the *Reds* and *Oranges* and lower it in the *Greens* and *Yellows* as shown. After these settings in the HSL tab, you should have an interesting looking technicolour effect!

5 **RECOLOUR THE HIGHLIGHTS.** Now click on the *Split-toning* tab next to the HSL/Grayscale tab and move down under the Highlights heading. Set the Saturation to *30* and then move the Hue slider to add a toning effect to the light parts of the image. Warmer highlights tend to work best, but just see what suits your image. Here, we went for an orange colour, setting Hue to *35*.

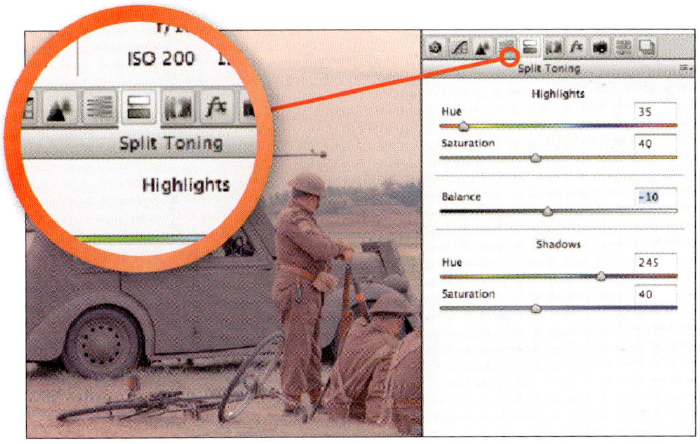

6 **RECOLOUR THE SHADOWS.** Next it's time to add a similar effect to the shadows, so move down the tab to that heading. Again, set the Saturation to around *30* and move the Hue slider - we've gone for some cooler shadows here using a blue colour with the Hue set to *245*. Finally, tweak the Balance slider to bias the effect towards the highlights at the left of the shadows at the right (*-10* here).

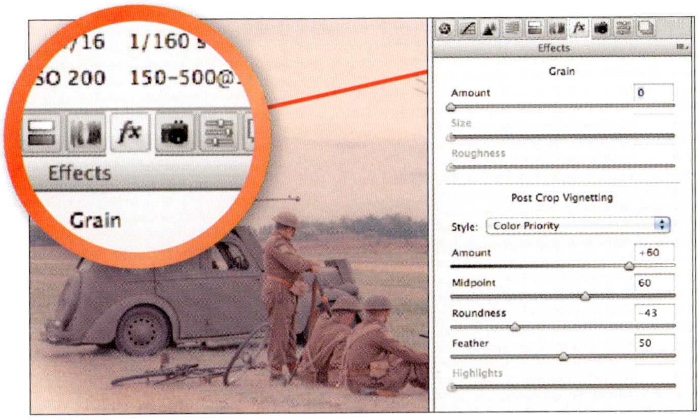

7 **ADD A VIGNETTE.** To finish off, we'll add a vignette. On some pics, darker edges work, but here a lightening of the corners is what we're after. Click on the *FX* tab and under *Post Crop Vignette*, pick *Color Priority*. Move the Amount slider to *+60* (a negative setting will darken the edges) and then alter the position and shape of the vignette to suit with the *Midpoint, Roundness* and *Feather* sliders.

8 FINISH **ADD SOME GRAIN.** A dusting of grain will also suit the vintage effect, so under *Grain*, set Amount to *30*. Size, which controls the size of the individual 'grains' can be moved up to around *50* and Roughness, which controls the contrast within the Noise, can also be set to *50*. For all three, higher values will give coarser images. Finally, hit *Open Image* to complete your retro conversions.

SAVE YOUR VINTAGE EFFECT AS A RAW RECIPE

Once you've created your vintage photo effect recipe, there's a good chance that you'll want to apply it to other images in your collection. To do it, click on the fly-out menu next to the Tabs and pick the option marked *Save Settings...*

You'll then be prompted to tick which settings you want to save (see the list on the right), so make sure that all the ones you want to apply are ticked. For example, here we've ticked the majority of them, including the *HSL Adjustments, Split Toning, Post Crop Vignette* and *Grain* boxes. However, it's a good idea to untick the settings input under the *Basic* tab as these will vary more widely from image to image. Now click *Save* and you'll be prompted to give a name to your effect, so type that in and hit *OK*.

Now, when you load up any image, you'll be able to click on the Presets tab and choose the effect you save from the list. It's a great way to save time when applying creative effects to your RAWs, so make sure you give it a try.

ADVANCED RAW SKILLS

VIDEO LESSON ON THE COVER DISC!

Ps

USE THE ADJUSTMENT BRUSH AND GRADUATED FILTER TOOLS TO CONVERT RAWS LIKE A PRO

WE'VE SEEN HOW a RAW file can be converted a number of times and blended together to give different exposure and contrast effects to different parts of the scene, but imagine how great it would be if you could do all this in one single RAW conversion! Well, provided you have the full version of Photoshop (CS4 or higher), you can! It's all made possible thanks to the Adjustment Brush, which allows you to apply different RAW conversion settings to different areas of an image. On top of that, there's also a nifty tool that applies a graduated filter effect, so in this tutorial, we'll explore both and see how you can make dramatic changes to exposure, colour and contrast in different parts of your pictures in one fell swoop...

THE START IMAGE

FILENAME
SANDSEND.DNG
The pic used in this technique is included on the cover disc, so have a practise and then try it out on your own images.

THE FINAL IMAGE
Considering the rough starting point, this seaside scene has polished up rather well in RAW, with a perfect balance to the exposure and contrast.

1 **START STRAIGHTEN THE RAW.** Open *SANDSEND.dng* into Photoshop CS4 or higher, and it'll load into Camera Raw. The first thing we need to address is the wonky horizon, so select the *Straighten tool* from the Toolbar, and drag the mouse along the horizon from the left. Release the mouse on the right of the horizon and the image will straighten up. Double-click to see the squared-up image.

2 **BRIGHTEN THE FOREGROUND.** We need to get the foreground looking better as it's currently under-exposed, so move the *Exposure* slider to the right until the foreground's lighting has improved. On our image, we ramped up the *Exposure* to *+1.80* – nearly two stops above our in-camera setting. Your sky will bleach out when you do this, but don't worry, as we can bring it back.

3 **ADD A HINT OF WARMTH.** The image is looking a little cool at the default White Balance setting, so move the *Temperature* slider up to around *6500* to warm things up. With that done, click on the *Adjustment Brush* (or hit the shortcut *K*) and with *New* selected at the top of the palette, move the *Exposure* slider down to about *-1.50*. Nothing will change, as we haven't used the brush yet.

4 **USE THE ADJUSTMENT BRUSH.** At the bottom of the palette, set *Feather, Flow* and *Density* to *100*, and then set *Size* so the brush covers half the height of the sky (*14* on our pic). Now paint over the sky, and run the brush down so the feathered edge touches the horizon. The sky will darken, thanks to the new *Exposure* value we've applied to the painted area. Tick *Show Mask* and you'll see it.

5 **ADJUST THE BRUSH.** It's called the *Adjustment Brush* for a good reason, because we can now apply further changes to the area covered by it. We need our sky to be a bit darker, so move the *Exposure* slider to the left until the pic looks nicely balanced. We went for *-2.00*, and to give the clouds more stand-out, we then ramped up the *Contrast* to *+50*. We left all the other sliders set to *0*.

6 **APPLY A GRAD FILTER EFFECT.** To give a traditional look and further darken the top of the sky, select the *Graduated Filter* (*G*) and set the Exposure to *-1.00*, and all the other sliders to 0. Click on the very top of the image and drag downwards to the top of the groynes, and you'll see the green and red dashed lines that indicate the start and finish of the graduated effect.

7 **TWEAK THE SETTINGS.** With the main changes made, return to the regular interface by clicking on the *Hand tool*, and you can now fine-tune your conversion, adjusting all the effects you've created along with the image itself. To get a bit more detail into the foreground, push *Fill Light* up to around *30*, and then to prevent it looking too washed out, boost *Blacks* to *10* to thicken the shadows.

8 FINISH **REDUCE THE GRAD STRENGTH.** We're just about there, now, but the grad is looking a little unnatural at the top. To reduce its strength, hit G to select the *Graduated Filter* again and click on one of the small circles to make the grad editable. Move the *Exposure* slider back to about *-0.60* to soften the effect, and then hit *Open Image* to load the picture into the standard interface of Photoshop.

USING MULTIPLE ADJUSTMENTS & GRADS

To keep things as versatlie as possible, you can use several different Adjustment Brushes and Graduated Filters, all with different effects. Above, we've used three grads to subtly enhance the sky, and on the left, you can see the 'pins' of five different *Adjustment Brushes* to fine-tune the *Exposure* and *Contrast* settings over the scene. The beauty of multiple localised adjustments like this is that you can work on particular sections within an image with each tool, rather than trying to make a complex alteration over the whole scene with just one grad or Adjustment Brush.

To create a new *Adjustment Brush*, simply hit *K* and then ensure that *New* is selected at the top of the palette. For a new *Graduated Filter*, hit *G* and drag on the image. In both cases, you'll need to avoid clicking on any existing adjustment pins that are present, as this will take you into the editing mode on that particular pin, and allow you to further alter it.

CHAPTER 5
FILTER EFFECTS

LEARN HOW TO ADD CREATIVE EFFECTS TO YOUR IMAGES

Remember, when you see this icon, there's a video lesson of the technique on the cover DVD.

P126 **MAKE A PHOTO PLANET**

Use the curiously named Polar Coordinates filter to create this unique and eyecatching effect. It's sure to get your friends wondering how you achieved it!

P110 **ADD ATTRACTIVE DEPTH-OF-FIELD EFFECTS**

Give your portraits a professional look by adding a pleasing blur to the background in Photoshop.

LEARN WITH US!

FILTERS ARE AN INTEGRAL PART OF PHOTOSHOP'S ARMOURY, AND THEY OFFER CREATIVE AND SATISFYING WAYS TO CHANGE THE LOOK OF YOUR PICTURES...

P122 CREATE A DRAMATIC LENS FLARE EFFECT & ADD IT TO A SCENE

Add a digital 'sun' and some virtual sunbeams with Filters and Layers to transform a backlit woodland picture into a magical image.

P114 GET A WATERCOLOUR LOOK BY BLENDING DIFFERENT FILTERS

Reduce an image to a simple line art state with one filter, apply a watercolour wash with another, then finish the whole thing off with a realistic hand-painted border and blend them all together.

P118 ADD DYNAMIC ZOOM BLUR

You can make action pics look more energetic than they really are by using our clever technique and placing the blur just where you want it for the best effect!

THE KEY TO SUCCESSFUL EFFECTS LIES IN THE WAY YOU CHOOSE AND BLEND FILTERS

IN THIS CHAPTER you'll get to see a selection of very different filter effects in action, and if you try them all using the start images on the disc, you'll start to see how varied and exciting the effects of filters can be. Take a look at the Filter menu in Photoshop or Elements though, and you'll be met by a daunting range of options, so getting started on the path to good results can be quite a trial with so many choices on offer. The thing is, filters can make or break a picture, so we've concentrated on the techniques that'll help you do the first bit, and avoid the second, as nobody wants the filter taking over and smothering the content of the picture itself!

Blending filters

In most cases, great results with filters come not from applying a single option, but from blending the effects of two or more filters together. The key to successful special effects lies in the way you choose and blend filters, so you won't be surprised to discover that all of our techniques use multiple Layers to produce the final image.

None of these projects are difficult to achieve, though, and as always, you'll find a helping hand in the videos on the disc.

VIDEO LESSON ON THE COVER DISC!

When you see this logo, it means there's an in-depth video lesson on our cover disc that accompanies the technique. Watch and learn as one of our experts takes you through the project, step by step!

ADD SHALLOW DEPTH-OF-FIELD EFFECTS TO YOUR PICS

GET THE PRO LOOK WITH ANY PORTRAIT BY ADDING A PLEASING BLUR TO THE BACKGROUND

IF THERE'S ONE THING THAT'S sure to characterise a professional looking portrait, it's a shallow depth-of-field look – one where the subject of your shot is pin sharp while the background diffuses into a pleasing blur. This gives the picture separation and allows you to remove distracting elements behind the person you're shooting, but it's not easily achieved on compact cameras, and can be tricky even on some D-SLRs. Fortunately this look is easy to apply in Photoshop, using effects found within the Filter menu. Turn over to see how it's done...

THE START IMAGE

FILE NAME AGATHA.DNG

The start image used in this technique can be found in the *Start Images* folder on the cover disc. Just open it up into Photoshop or Elements and run through the lesson. Once you've had a practice and watched the accompanying video, try it with your own pictures.

VIDEO LESSON ON THE COVER DISC!

Ps Pse

THE FINAL IMAGE

We've added increasing amounts of blur to the picture, giving a high-end, professional look to this portrait.

START ADDING BELIEVABLE BLUR EFFECTS

In this technique you'll discover a smart way to add a blur effect to your pictures in Photoshop or Elements, achieving the kind of shallow depth-of-field effect characterised by professional-looking portraits.

Using this effect on portrait images will really help your subject stand out from the background, but once you've learnt how to do it, you can use it on any type of picture you like, and while it's something that can be achieved in camera by shooting at very wide aperture settings, sometimes you just can't get enough blur this way, so it's sensible to understand how the effect can be added digitally.

GET A SHALLOW DEPTH-OF-FIELD EFFECT THAT LOOKS JUST LIKE THE REAL THING...

Although the example picture we're using – *Agatha.jpg* which you'll find on the cover disc – was shot at quite a wide aperture and the background has blurred a little, we want to take this a bit further and to soften some of the details that are still there. By the end, we'll achieve a pleasing shallow-focus effect and one that's almost indistinguishable from the 'real thing'. We'll show you how to build up the blurred effect using multiple Layers, which will add depth and realism to the effect and soon, you'll have a great finished picture.

So, it's Photoshop's Filter menu to the rescue, again, but as always if you want top results, it's not as simple as just clicking an on-screen button. Principally we'll be using Photoshop's Gaussian blur filter, but also combining this with another filter called Fragment, to improve the effect and make it look more natural. If you have the full version of Photoshop, it's a good idea to use *Lens Blur* instead (it's also found under the *Filter→Blur* menu but isn't featured in Elements), as this gives the most realistic look possible (see below for more).

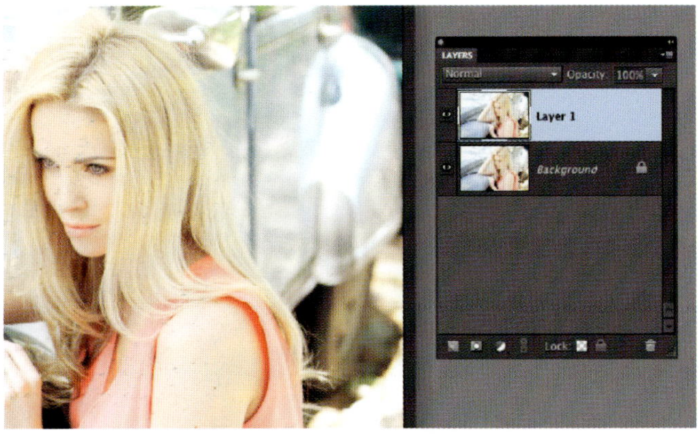

1 START OPEN & DUPLICATE THE LAYER. From the cover disc, open the image called *AGATHA.jpg* and then bring your Layers palette onto the screen with *Window→ Layers*. We want to keep some parts of the scene sharp, like the subject's eyes, so we need to keep an unblurred version of the picture and work on a duplicate. Go to *Layer→ New→ Layer via Copy* or press *Ctrl+J* on the keyboard.

2 FRAGMENT THE NEW LAYER. In the Layers palette, you'll now have *Layer 1* as well as the *Background* Layer, so making sure that this new Layer is highlighted, go to *Filter→Pixellate→ Fragment*. Zoom in close and you'll now see a sort of double image as though the picture was slightly out of focus. It's still a bit too sharp though, so we'll smooth out the effect in the next step.

3 ADD SOME GAUSSIAN BLUR. With *Layer 1* still highlighted in the Layers palette (if it's not just click the Layer thumbnail) go back up to the Filter menu and this time go to *Filter→ Blur→ Gaussian Blur*. Input a Radius setting of *1.5px* and click *OK*. You'll notice the effect of the *Fragment* filter soften slightly, giving it a look much more like the blur you get from shooting with a wide aperture in-camera.

4 ADD A LAYER MASK. The whole of Layer 1 is still blurred, but we want some parts of the subject to be sharp, so now it's time to pick out those areas. To do it, go into the Layers palette and click on the *Add Layer Mask* icon (a circle inside a rectangle). You'll see a white rectangle appear by the side of *Layer 1* (the Layer Mask) and we'll paint into this to control where the sharp areas of the picture will be.

5 **PAINT INTO THE MASK.** Pick the *Brush tool* (*B*) from the Toolbox and click on the *Presets* menu in the Options bar. Pick a *200px* soft brush and, making sure the tool's Opacity is set to *100%* in the Options bar, and that you're painting Black (press *D* then *X*), run it over the subject's eyes to reveal the sharpness from the Layer below. Drop the Opacity to *20%* and paint a little more for a soft join.

6 **ADD SOME MORE BLUR.** The further the scenery is from the the subject, the more it should blur, so we need to strengthen the effect there. Copy *Layer 1*, by pressing *Ctrl+J* (its Mask will copy, too) then repeat the two filters from Steps *2* and *3*, this time increasing the amount of Gaussian blur to *5px*. In the Mask, paint Black over the subject's hair to knock back the blur in those parts.

7 **INCREASE THE BLUR.** Add another layer of blur, hitting *Ctrl+J* again to copy the layer, then apply the filters as before, but this time increase the blur Radius to *10px*. Again the mask from the last Layer will be copied over, so paint into that, removing the effect from the subject's hand and shoulder. Add one last layer of blur (*20px*), this time masking more broadly around the subject and you're done.

8 **FINISH SHARPEN THE EYES.** The subject's eyes and face are now very much at the heart of the pic, but just to make sure, let's sharpen them. In the Layers palette, click the Background Layer and then go to *Enhance→ Unsharp Mask* (*Filter→ Sharpen→ Unsharp Mask* in Photoshop). Input an Amount of *100*, Radius *1.0* and Threshold *0*. Click *OK*, then go to *Layer→ Flatten Image* and you're done.

TRY IT USING THE LENS BLUR FILTER IN PHOTOSHOP

THE LENS BLUR FILTER

The two filters used to create the blur in the technique above are designed to give a more lifelike and defocused look to the blurred areas. But if you've got the full version of Photoshop, rather than Elements, you'll have access to the *Lens Blur* filter which can do an even better job. To use it instead, simply replace the *Fragment* and *Gaussian blur* steps with *Filter→ Blur→ Lens Blur*.

In the *Lens blur* palette you'll be confronted with a lot of options, but you only need to use a few of the sliders to get a great effect. Under the *Iris* heading, first set the Shape to either *Hexagon, Heptagon, or Octagon*, and the *Blade Curvature* to around *30* to give the blur the most realistic shape possible.

Next, just drag the *Radius* slider to the right until you get the amount of blur you want and hit *OK*. For each Layer you add in the technique, increase the amount of blur a little and you'll achieve a nice, natural-looking blurred effect. That's all there is to it!

PEN & WASH EFFECTS

GET THAT WATERCOLOUR LOOK WITH ANY IMAGE

NO ONE CAN resist the urge to turn their pics into paintings, and this technique makes it nice and easy to achieve. The problem is, if you go straight to the *Filter* menu and start applying painterly-sounding effects in their standard state, you tend to get disappointing results that bear little or no resemblance to the description.

It's actually by blending different filter effects together that you get the best finish, and in this technique we're going to first reduce a picture to a simplified line art state with one filter, and then apply a watercolour wash to it with another. Finally, we'll create a hand-painted border to give a real human feel to it, and disguise the fact that we started with a digital photo!

THE START IMAGE

FILENAME
RYDAL.JPG
The pic used in this technique is included on the cover disc, so have a practice before trying it out on your own images.

VIDEO LESSON ON THE COVER DISC!

Ps Pse

THE FINAL IMAGE
We've blended different filters together and created a new sky from scratch to give our photo a painterly feel.

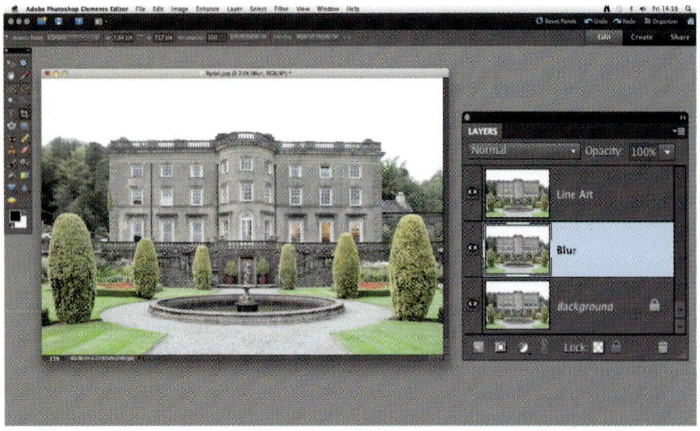

1 START **MAKE TWO COPY LAYERS.** Open *Rydal.jpg* into Photoshop or Elements and hit *Ctrl+J* twice to make two copies of the *Background* Layer. You'll see the copies stacked up in the *Layers palette* if you go to *Window→ Layers*. Double-click on the words of the top Layer so they're highlighted and type in *Line Art*, then rename the middle Layer to *Blur* in the same way.

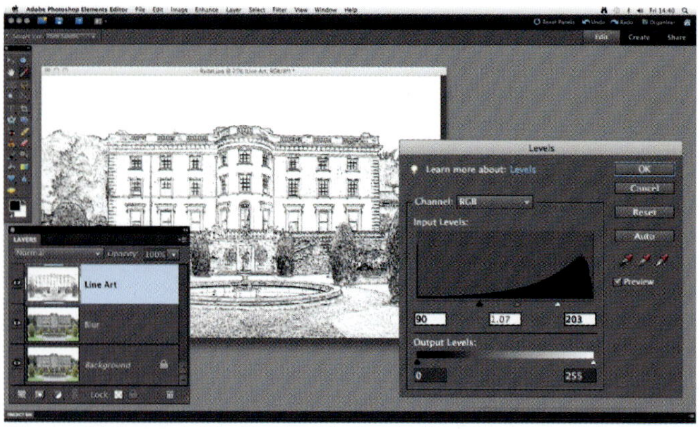

2 **CREATE A SKETCH EFFECT.** Click on your *Line Art* Layer at the top of the stack and go to *Filter→ Stylize→ Find Edges*. Once the filter has run, hit *Ctrl+Shift +U* to turn it to mono. This gives you a simplified picture, but to improve it, open *Levels* (*Ctrl+L*) and move the sliders to get a crisp sketch effect. On our image, the *Levels* settings were *90, 1.07,* and *203*, but the settings will be different for your images.

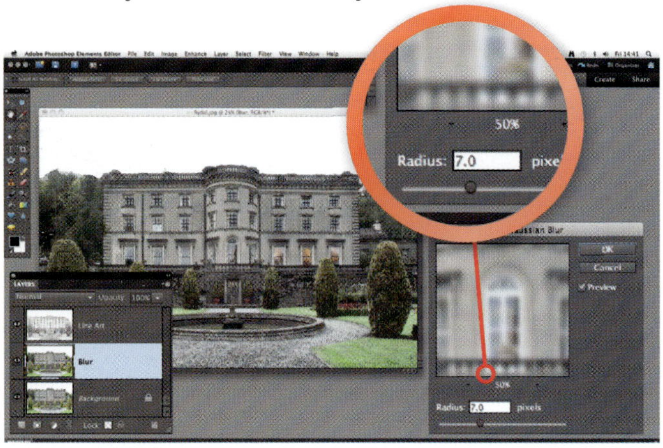

3 **BLEND AND BLUR.** Now you have a line art version, click where it says *Normal* in the *Layers palette* and change the Blending Mode to *Multiply*. This will blend the Line Art Layer with the one beneath. Now click on the Blur Layer to make it active, and go to *Filter→ Blur→ Gaussian blur*. We used a *Radius* of *7.0 pixels*. Our watercolour is taking shape, but the bland white sky needs fixing.

4 **CREATE A NEW SKY.** Hit *D* to set black & white as the default colours, then click on the foreground colour swatch and pick a sky blue from the *Color Picker*. Click *OK* and then select the *Rectangular Marquee tool*. Click on the top Layer in the *Layers palette*, then on the *Create a new Layer* icon, then draw a Selection in the sky area. Go to *Filter→ Render→ Clouds* and you'll have some virtual sky.

5 **MAKE YOUR SKY FIT.** Hit *Ctrl+T* to enter *Transform*, untick *Constrain Proportions* in the Options bar (Elements only) and drag your digital cloudscape out to fill the whole of the sky. You'll find you'll get a more natural perspective if you hold *Ctrl* and pull the top corner handles outwards at the top. Once you've covered the blank area, hit *Return* to confirm the changes, and *Ctrl+D* to lose the 'marching ants'.

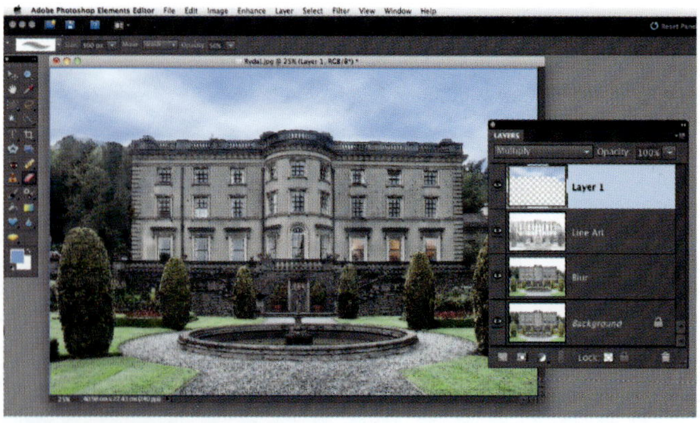

6 **TIDY UP THE SKY.** Your new sky will cover the top of the building, but change the Blending Mode to *Multiply*, and the structure will show through. Pick up the *Eraser tool* and in the Options bar at the top of the screen, choose a *300px*, soft-edged brush. Drop the *Opacity* to around *50%*, and then dab away at the overlapping sky areas until you've got rid of them and maintained a natural blend.

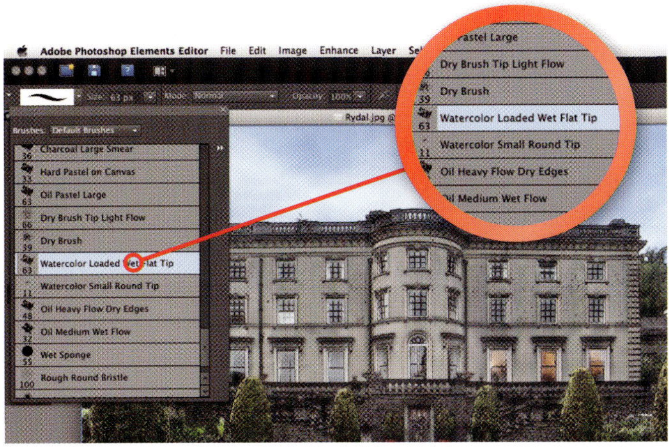

7 SET UP YOUR BRUSH. We're nearly there now, but because watercolours seldom have a squared-off edge, we need to 'humanize' the border if we're genuinely going for a pen & wash effect. To do this, create a new Layer at the top of the stack, and then hit *D* then *X* to set white as the foreground colour. For the right sort of brush, pick *Watercolor Loaded Wet Flat Tip* from the brush picker.

8 FINISH PAINT AN ARTY BORDER. Use an *Opacity* of about *35%*, and dab away around the edge of the pic, building up a natural, hand-painted border effect. When you're happy, save the file in Photoshop format, as this will preserve the Layers, and even allow you to use your carefully created border Layer on a different image. Now it's done, you can simply drag it onto another picture!

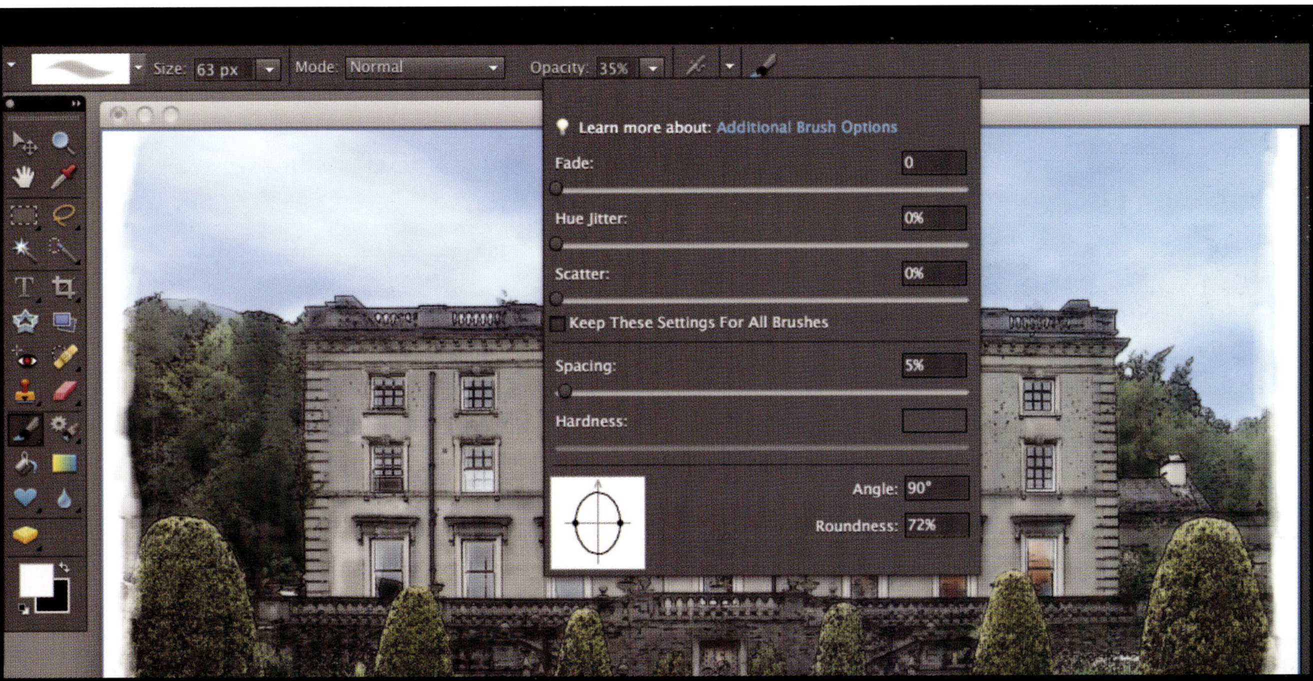

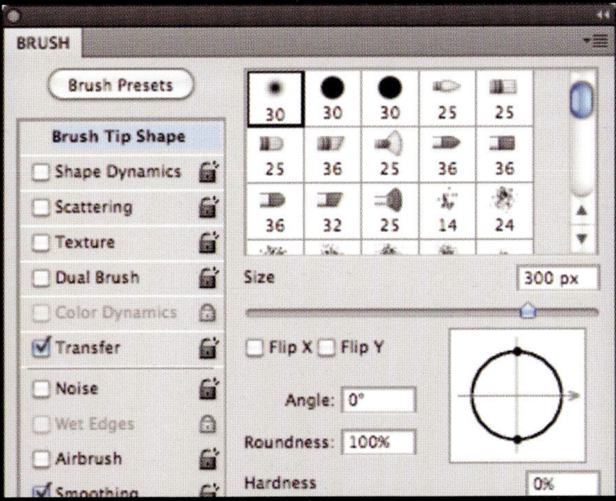

TAKING CONTROL OF YOUR BRUSH HEAD ANGLE IN PHOTOSHOP

When painting arty borders with anything other than round brushes, you'll find that you'll often want to change the angle of the brush when you work along the horizontal edges at the top and bottom of the picture. One option is to rotate the whole thing by going to *Image→ Rotate→ 90° Right* (*Image→ Image Rotation > 90° Right* in Photoshop), but a neater way that gives more control is to adjust the angle of the brush head itself.

In Elements, click on the *Brush* icon at the right of the icons along the Options bar, and you can rotate the arrow at the bottom of the palette to get the brush head at any angle you like. In Photoshop, go to *Window > Brush* (or hit the shortcut F5) and with *Brush Tip Shape* highlighted, you can turn the arrow to set the brush head exactly how you want it.

ADD DYNAMIC ZOOM BLUR

LEARN HOW TO MAKE ACTION PICS LOOK MORE ENERGETIC THAN EVER

THE TRADITIONAL technique for making a zoom blur or 'zoom burst' picture with a film camera was to use a longer-than-normal exposure, and then zoom out while the camera's shutter was open. This recorded the movement of the zoom as streaks of colour, and when you got the pics back a week later, you'd then find out whether or not you'd made a hash of it! With digital capture, of course, you get to find out much faster whether your zoom burst technique has worked effectively, but if you don't fancy taking this trial and error approach with a camera and a zoom lens, then there's a much easier way to produce this dynamic, action-packed effect. In Photoshop or Elements, you can control the position and intensity of your zoom burst, and what's more, you can fine-tune the results using Layers to cook up some truly stunning effects. And the best bit is, you always get the zoom blur where you want it, and you get to brush away the parts you want to remain sharp.

VIDEO LESSON ON THE COVER DISC!

Ps Pse

THE START IMAGE

FILENAME CYCLIST.JPG The pic already has some movement as it's a panning shot taken with a burst of flash, but it'd be great to give it more using our zoom blur effect. It's on the disc if you want to load it up and practice the technique.

THE FINAL IMAGE

Who says pictures have to be sharp? Our zoom blur effect gives a really dynamic finish that's bursting with energy and movement, and it's really easy to do!

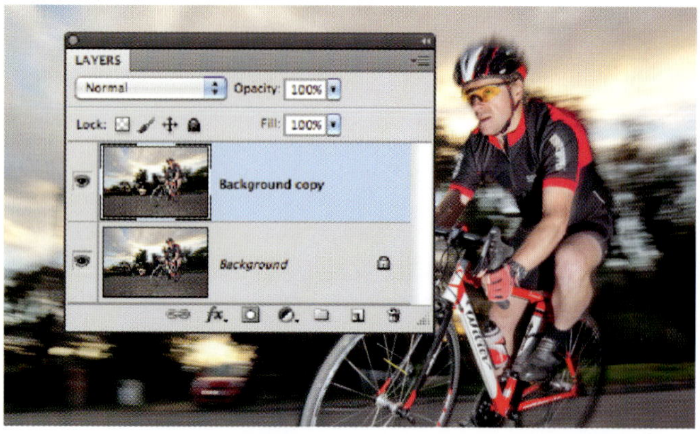

1 **START MAKE A COPY LAYER.** Open *Cyclist.jpg* into Photoshop or Elements, or even better, pick a sporty or dynamic image of your own. Once it's up on screen, open your *Layers palette* (*Window→ Layers*) and drag the *Background* Layer onto the *Create a new Layer* icon at the bottom of the palette to duplicate it. You'll see a *Background Copy* Layer appear at the top of the Layers stack.

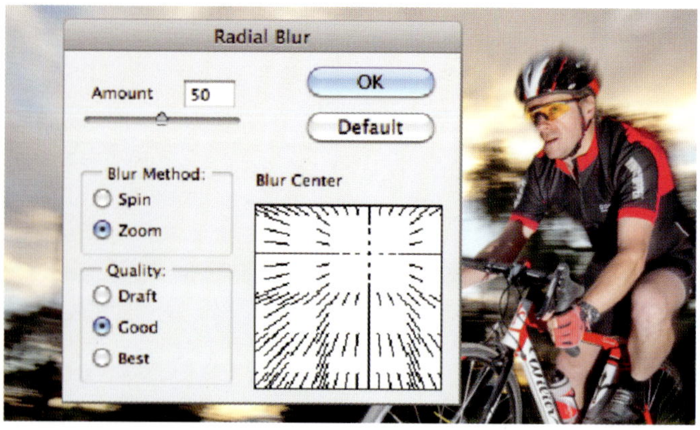

2 **CREATE A ZOOM BURST EFFECT.** With the top Layer active in the *Layers palette*, go to *Filter→ Blur→* Radial Blur, and the dialog box will pop up on screen. Set *Amount* to about *50*, and under *Blur Method*, select *Zoom*. Use *Good* under the *Quality* setting, and then click in the upper-right area of the *Blur Center* box. Now hit *OK*, and see where your blur centre has ended up on your image.

3 **ADJUST AND REFINE THE POSITION.** On our example pic, you want the centre of the zoom to appear over the face, and chances are, you won't get it right first time. Check where your blur centre is on the pic, and then hit *Ctrl+Z* to undo the effect and go to *Filter→ Blur→ Radial Blur* again. Click on the box to reposition the effect, hit *OK* and see if you're a bit closer. See the panel on the right for more.

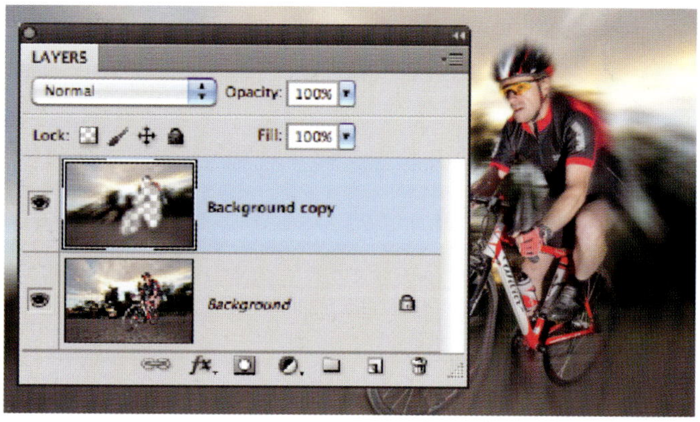

4 **REMOVE THE BLUR SELECTIVELY.** It'll take you a few goes to get the blur in exactly the right place, but once you've got it right, the hardest part is behind you! Pick up the *Eraser tool*, and in the Options bar at the top of the screen, set *Opacity* to *50%*. Now, with a soft-edged brush about *300px* in size, gently dab away at the face, chest and tyres to reveal the clean image from the Layer beneath.

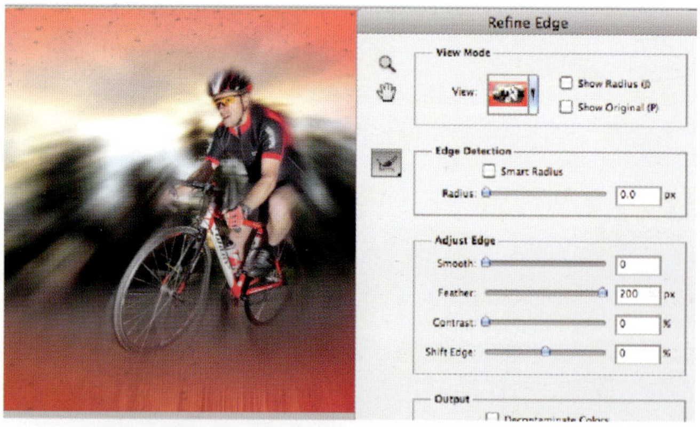

5 **SELECT THE EDGE.** The image is taking shape, but to enhance our effect, we need to help draw the attention to the zoom burst's centre, and a great way to do this is to darken the edges of the image with a vignette. With the *Lasso tool*, draw around the pic so you have a ragged margin, and then click the *Refine Edge* button and move *Feather* to around *200px* to soften the edge. Click *OK*.

6 **DARKEN THE VIGNETTE.** Now hit *Ctrl+Shift+I* to select the outside area rather than the inside, and then click the Adjustment Layer icon at the foot of the *Layers palette*. Choose *Levels* from the list and move the black point and mid-point sliders a little to the right. You'll see the edge darken. If you're using an older version of the software, click *OK*, but if you have no *OK* button, just carry on!

7 **BOOST THE COLOUR.** We're just about home now, but the image could do with a bit more punch to emphasise the vibrancy of the sunset and the cyclist's clothes. To liven up the colours, click the *Adjustment Layer* icon once more and this time, select *Hue/Saturation* from the list. In the palette, move the *Saturation* slider up to about *+25*, and watch those colours come to life.

8 FINISH **FINE-TUNE THE EFFECT.** The image is looking great, but if you want to adjust the intensity of the vignette or the colours - no problem! Because Adjustment Layers have been used for both these steps, we can simply double-click on the *Adjustment Layer* thumbnail in the *Layers palette*, and change the *Levels* settings on the vignette or the *Saturation* amount on the colour boost.

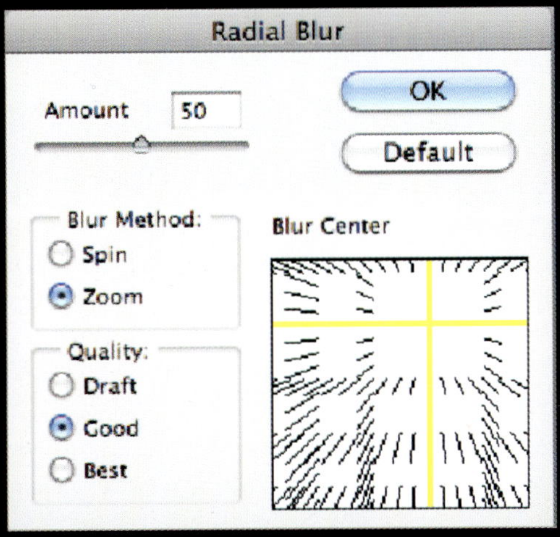

ACCURATE POSITIONING OF ZOOM BLUR EFFECTS

What doesn't make life easy is the fact that the Radial Blur's dialog box features a square preview window, and most pics you use will of course be rectangles! This makes the correct positioning of the blur centre a bit of a 'hit and miss' exercise, but provided you use a copy Layer and make a mental note of what you need to do, we reckon you'll get it spot on in three attempts (or four at the most!).

The trick is to convert the position you want on your pic into a kind of 10x10 grid reference. In our example below, the face is about 6/10ths along the horizontal axis of the pic, and about 8/10ths up the vertical. If we then apply this '6 along and 8 up' to the square format of the preview window in the Radial Blur dialog (left), we get pretty close to the position we want. Once you've clicked OK, you can see the exact spot of the blur centre on the pic, so all you need to do is make a mental note of what you need to do (such as 'up a bit and a little to the right'). Transfer this to the square preview on your next attempt, and you'll be there!

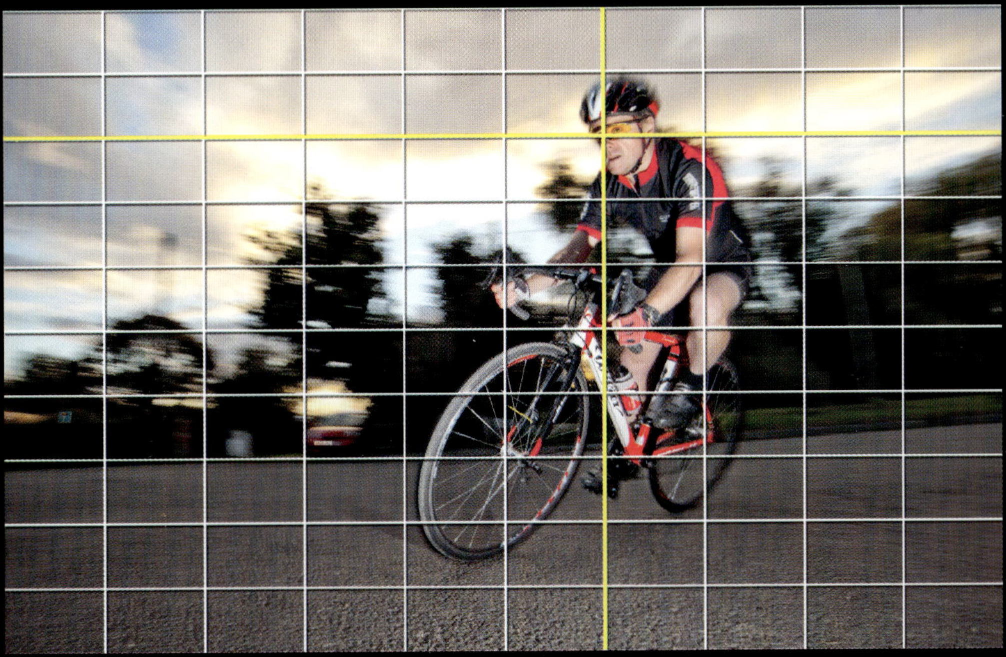

MAKING A BEST GUESS TO POSITION YOUR ZOOM BLUR

Though you wouldn't go so far as to create an actual grid on the image, you can see the principle behind the grid reference system here. By estimating how far along and how far up the picture you want the centre of your zoom blur to be, it becomes easier to pinpoint the right spot on the square preview image in the Radial Blur dialog box.

Without using this system, you can be there for quite a while trying to convert a rectangular image into a square format in your head! On our image, the subject's face is situated around 6 along and 8 up if we divide it into tenths. Simply transfer these coordinates to the preview window, and you'll be pretty close to the right spot. Give it a try next time you're creating a zoom blur effect, and you'll be surprised how much easier it makes the process.

ADD LENS FLARE EFFECTS

INJECT SOME SUNSHINE INTO ANY BACKLIT IMAGE

ONE OF THE FANTASTIC things about digital imaging is it can take your pictures in entirely new directions. This often means that pictures that don't quite make the grade can be reinvented and turned into portfolio pieces, simply by adding some new elements. The *Filter* menu is a great place to start your journey when looking for a new direction, and with a little practice, you can soon find an approach that will pay off.

If you've got a backlit image - like our woodland shot - a great way to pep it up is to introduce a sunny 'hotspot' via a special filter called *Lens Flare*. As well as giving a burnt-out centre point, this emulates the internal reflections that occur within a lens when you shoot into a strong light source.

The effect is very cinematic, but can be really effective if you want to inject some 'heightened reality' into a scene. This woodland landscape is perfect for the technique, and in the step-by-step we'll not only add some lens flare, but will also create some attractive sunbeams breaking through the trees to give a really atmospheric effect. Check out the rather flat-looking start image below, and we think the enhanced result is a lot more successful in making you want to be there!

THE START IMAGE

FILENAME WOODLAND.JPG
The picture used in this technique is included on the cover disc, so have a practice before trying it out on your own images.

THE FINAL IMAGE
We've used various filters to produce the sunlight and sunbeam effects, and the result is an attractive, dreamlike image.

1 START **CREATE A BLACK LAYER.** Open *Woodland.jpg* then get your *Layers palette* on screen by going to *Window→ Layers.* Press *D* on the keyboard to set the default colours to black and white, and then click on the *Create a New Layer* icon. To fill the new Layer with black, hit *Alt+Backspace*, and then in the *Layers palette*, click where it says *Normal* and change the Blending Mode to *Screen.*

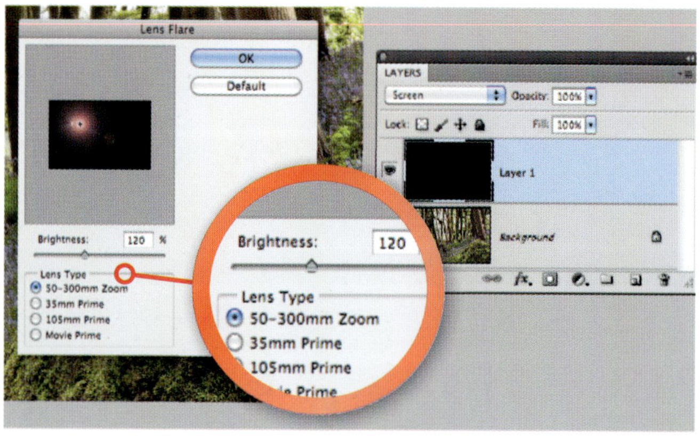

2 **USE THE LENS FLARE FILTER.** Go to *Filter→ Render→ Lens Flare* and in the dialog box, select the *50-300mm zoom* option, with the *Brightness* set to around *120.* Click on the preview window above to position the flare about two-thirds up and one-third in from the left. You'll see the shape of the flare so when you're happy, click *OK* and the lens flare effect will appear on your image.

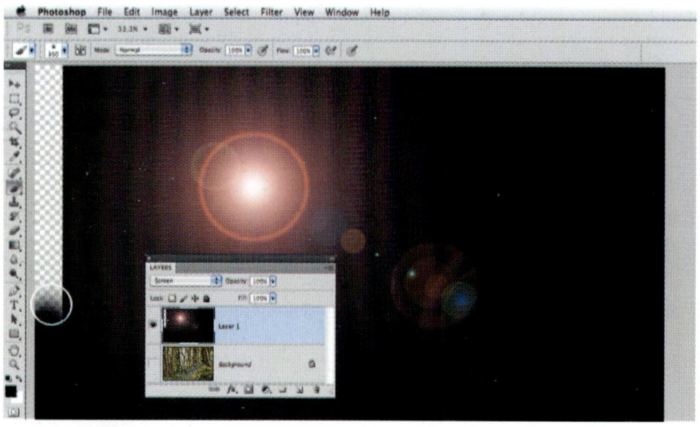

3 **POSITION YOUR NEW 'SUN'.** Select the *Move tool* and position the flare on the image so it falls between two trees. Switch off the *Background* Layer by clicking the 'eye' icon next to it. Now select a brush, hit *X* to make black the foreground colour, and then paint into any transparent areas round the edges on the Flare Layer. This will stop any chance of a hard line appearing on your pic.

4 **ADD SOME SUNBEAMS.** Switch the Background back on, then pick up the *Polygonal Lasso tool* and create a sunbeam shape by clicking on the flare centre and drawing a narrow triangle out to the edge of the image, and back to the starting point. Once you've done one, hold *Shift* and make another, and keep going until you have three or four triangular Selections emanating from the flare.

5 **SOFTEN THE SUNBEAMS.** At the foot of the *Layers palette*, click the *Adjustment Layer* icon and choose *Hue/Saturation* from the list. Move the *Lightness* slider to the right to around *+30*, and you'll see your 'sunbeams' appear. They're too hard-edged, though, so to soften them, go to *Filter→ Blur→ Gaussian Blur* and use a *Radius* of *10px.* Click *OK*, and they'll look better, but not yet realistic.

6 **PAINT IN A NATURAL LOOK.** To make the sunbeams more natural, click on the Mask next to the Adjustment Layer and pick a soft-edged brush about *150px* in size. In the Options bar, set *Opacity* to *30%* and paint black onto the sunbeams to break up the artificial look. Keep the strokes in line with the direction of the sunbeams and work away until you have a natural-looking result.

7 **INCREASE THE SATURATION.** To give an overall boost to the colours, click on the *Background* Layer and hit *Ctrl+J* to make a copy. Now go to *Filter→Blur→Gaussian Blur*, and use a *Radius* of *10px*. In the *Layers palette*, set the Blending Mode to *Color*, and then hit *Ctrl+U* and push *Saturation* to *+30*. Click *OK*. This method lets you increase *Saturation* smoothly without breaking up the image.

8 FINISH **DODGE THE SUNBEAMS.** To bring out the beams and foreground, hold *Alt* and go to *Layer→Merge visible* to crunch all your work into a new Layer. Select the *Dodge tool*, and in the Options bar, set *Range* to *Highlights* and *Exposure* to *5%*. Now play a soft-edged brush over the sunbeams and foreground to enhance them and add definition. Go to *Layer→Flatten image* when you're happy.

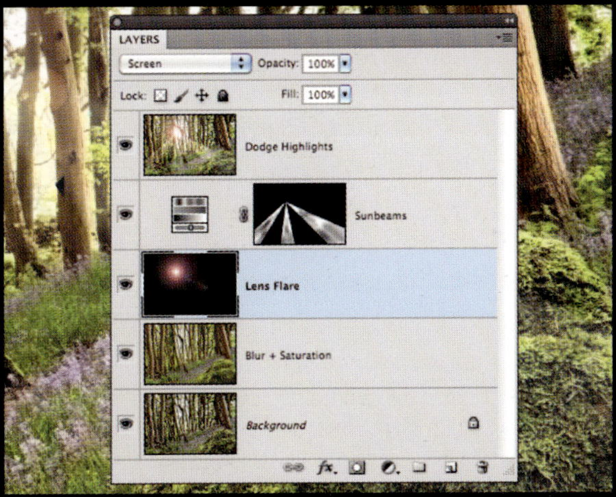

STAYING IN CONTROL OF THE LENS FLARE FILTER

You'll notice that we've placed the Lens Flare filter on a separate, black-filled Layer for this technique, and that's because it's an effect that can be hard to position and control with real accuracy.

Unlike with the 'hit and hope' approach of placing the *Radial Blur* filter, you do actually get a preview of the image itself when deciding on where to put the Lens Flare effect, but there are two downsides that come with this. First, the preview is very small, making precise positioning quite tricky, and second, the flare is embedded within the image, so it becomes fixed once you've clicked *OK*, and you can't do anything about it.

By placing the effect on a separate Layer, you have the full freedom to reposition or alter the Lens Flare, and that's essential for staying in control of your image. Use this Black Layer method whenever you opt for a bit of flare, and your imaging will run nice and smoothly.

THE FINAL IMAGE

By twisting a landscape into a circle you can create this incredible effect - and it's all thanks to the Filter menu.

MAKE AN AMAZING PHOTO PLANET

WIDE-ANGLE LENSES & PANORAMAS CAN ONLY TAKE YOU SO FAR – FOR A REALLY WIDE VIEW YOU NEED A PHOTO PLANET!

VIDEO LESSON ON THE COVER DISC!

Ps Pse

IF YOU'VE SEEN images like this before and wondered how they were created, now's your chance to find out, because in this lesson we'll show you how to create your own photo planet. Making a picture like this is all down to some clever preparation and an easy-to-use filter from Photoshop's extensive range but, as is often the case with Photoshop effects, finding the right filter can be difficult. You won't find anything in the menu that says 'Photo-planet' or 'Circular Panorama' - instead you'll need to make use of the mysteriously named *Polar Coodinates* - a filter that's designed to bend pictures in extreme ways. Read on to find out how it's done...

THE START IMAGE

FILE NAME ***BEACHHUTS.JPG***

This image is a great candidate for turning into a photo planet - the edges of the scene are reasonably similar, so there won't be too much distortion, and the main details run along the middle where the distortion will be at its least.

GET A SUPER-WIDE VIEW WITH A PHOTO PLANET

As a photographer you've probably experimented with wide-angle lenses or panoramic effects, so that you can pack in as much of a scene as possible - but if you want a really wide view, you have to give a photo planet effect a try! This filter recipe is dead easy to apply and the results are quite staggering, so it's one you'll definitely want to have a go at.

Here we'll be using the start image called *BEACH HUTS.jpg*, and twisting it into a tiny virtual world floating in the sky. It's on the cover disc for you to practise with, but once you've seen how easy it is to do, we bet you'll be bursting to try it out on one of your own shots! Just take a look at the tips on the opposite page to see which pictures will work best and why, and you'll be well on the way to making your own.

THIS FILTER RECIPE IS DEAD EASY TO APPLY AND THE RESULTS ARE STAGGERING

How to do it

So how do you go about making a photo planet? Well, there's no button to push, or specific option to tick - you just need to prepare the picture in the right way and use a fairly obscure filter to create the warping effect. That's what makes the *Filter* menu so intriguing - it's packed with amazing functions for you to try out on your digital pictures, but sometimes the most dramatic effects come from filters you'd never think of using.

To make this photo planet we'll be using the *Polar Coordinates* filter, found within the *Distort* sub-menu. It's certainly not one that springs from the menu to offer an obvious benefit, so you're unlikely to have tried it out before.

But when you see what the *Polar Coordinates* filter is capable of by completing this technique, you'll surely seek it out and want to give it a go.

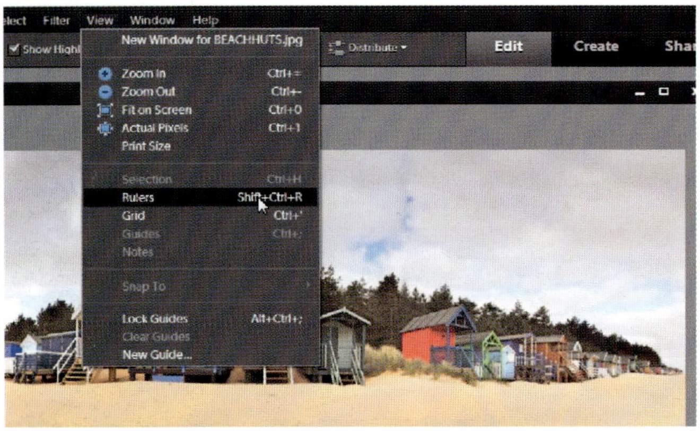

1 START OPEN & SET A GUIDE. Open the file called *BEACH HUTS.jpg* and before you get started let's make sure the picture will work correctly as a photo planet. For this to happen the edges need to be aligned, so press *Ctrl+Shift+R* (*Ctrl+R* in Photoshop) to activate the rulers and drag out a guide from the top one, down to run along the horizon. As you can see it doesn't quite line up.

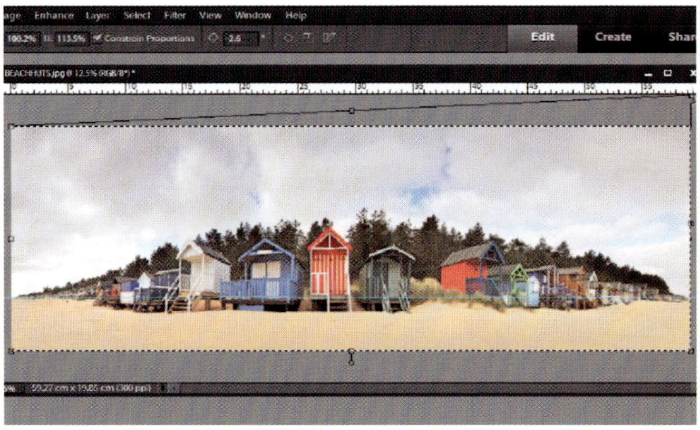

2 TRANSFORM THE HORIZON. To make the two edges of the horizon line up, press *Ctrl+A* to select the whole image, then *Ctrl+T* to enter *Free Transform* mode. Now hold down the *Ctrl* key and as you do, click and drag the top-right corner handle upwards, distorting the horizon so it lines up with the guide. Hit *Return* or click the green tick at the foot of the bounding box when you're done.

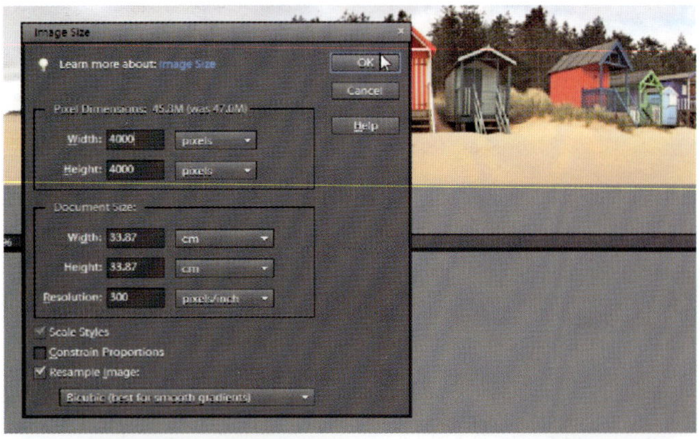

3 SQUARE UP THE PICTURE. The next thing you need to do is turn your image square (if you don't the finished 'planet' will look too distorted. To do it, go to *Image→ Resize→ Image Size* or press *Ctrl+Alt+I*. Now, making sure that *Constrain Proportions* is unticked within the palette, input *4000* pixels for both the *Width* and *Height*. Click *OK* and the image will be squished into a square shape.

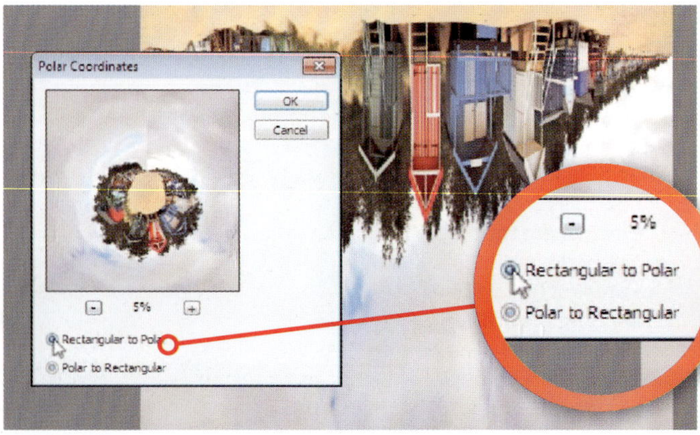

4 TURN IT INTO A PLANET. Now go to *Image→ Rotate→ 180°* (*Image→ Image Rotation→ 180°* in Photoshop), to flip the picture around. Now let's make the planet, so go to *Filter→ Distort→ Polar Coordinates*. In the palette that appears, click *Rectangular to Polar* and hit *OK*. The pic will now fold around in a circle and create the basic shape of the photo planet.

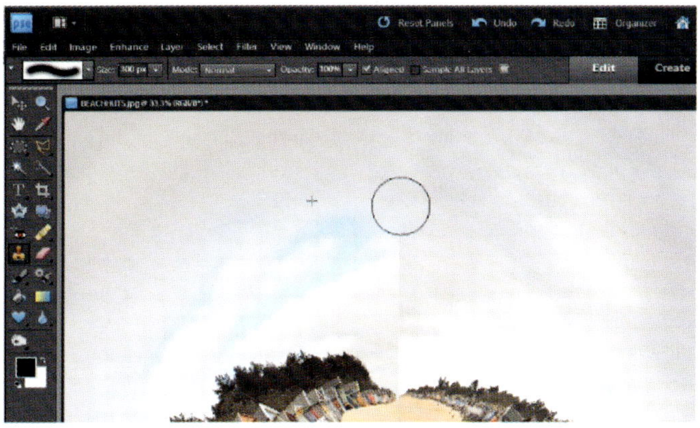

5 HIDE THE JOIN. You'll see a noticeable line running up through the image – the join between the wrapped edges – and this needs to be removed. To fix it, zoom in on the join area and pick the *Clone Stamp tool* from the Toolbox. Hold the *Alt* key and click on an area near the join, then paint those sampled pixels over the edge to hide. Keep doing this until the hard line is covered.

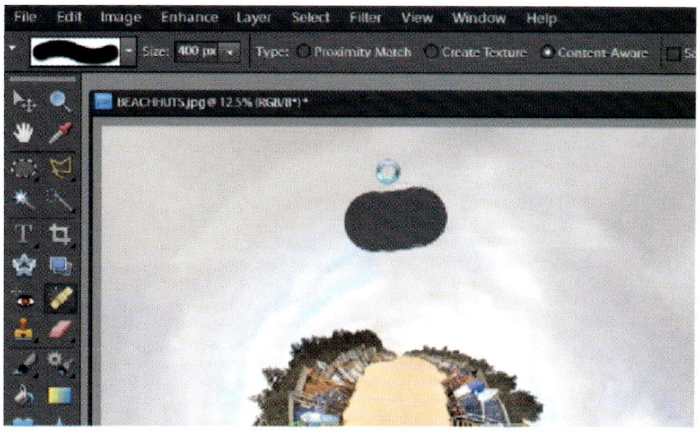

6 HEAL THE IMAGE. Rotate the image by 180° just as before, then to make sure the join looks as good as possible, zoom back in on it and pick the *Spot Healing Brush tool*. Run this over any 'rough' looking areas and you'll get a much nicer blend, but avoid using it on more complex details as in these it can give a soft and slightly fogged look which will seem out of place – use the *Clone Stamp tool* on those.

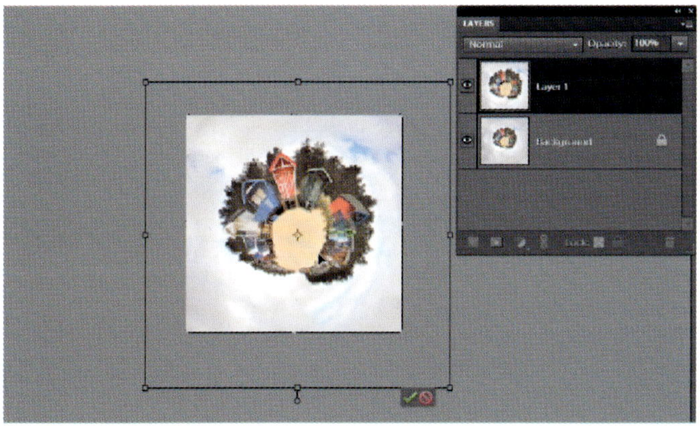

7 FIX THE SKY. You'll notice a few areas where the pixels have been stretched to fill the edges of the frame. Press *Ctrl+J* to duplicate the Layer, then *Ctrl+T* to enter *Free Transform* once more, then drag the corner handles out to enlarge the pic, until the 'good' sky meets the edge. To avoid distorting the picture, tick the *Constrain Proportions* box in the Options bar (the chain link icon in Photoshop).

8 FINISH DARKEN THE EDGES. To complete the effect, choose the *Elliptical Marquee tool* from the Toolbox and drag it out across the pic, then go to *Select→ Feather* and input *250px*. Next go to *Select→ Inverse* and open the *Levels palette* with *Ctrl+L*. Drag the Midpoint slider to the right and click *OK*. Finally, press *Ctrl+U* and move the *Saturation* slider to around *+30*. That's it!

WHAT PICTURES CAN YOU USE FOR A PHOTO PLANET?

Because the sides of the original picture are going to end up next to one another when they're warped into a photo planet, this technique works best on pictures where the sides of the picture look very similar.

In the first few steps we looked at levelling up the horizon to make sure there's not an obvious-looking step when the planet is made, but what you really need are subjects that match up, fairly consistently at either end of the image.

Some cloning of these areas is inevitable, but by selecting the right kind of images you'll save yourself a lot of work in the long run. You certainly don't want something large and detailed that's cut off by the edge of the frame, like the building in our example here, so either look for pictures in your own portfolio that sync up at the edges, or go out and shoot one, making sure to check the border of the picture. Once you give it a try you'll find it's certainly not as complicated as it sounds!

YOUR DVD

SLIP THE DVD INTO YOUR PC OR MAC AND FIND OUT WHY IT'S THE SMART WAY TO LEARN PHOTOSHOP...

Imagine having an expert Photoshop tutor all to yourself. One that never speaks too fast or glosses over important details. One you can stop, rewind and listen to, over and over again as many times as you like. And one that lets you practise on the very same images they're using in the lesson, so you can see every step happen 'live' on your computer.

Well, imagine no more, because that's exactly what you'll get from the *Ultimate Photoshop Course* DVD – a flexible and easy-to-follow Photoshop tutor on your PC screen! There are 28 separate video lessons on the DVD, adding up to an incredible six hours of first-class tuition, and each lesson is created by the award-winning team that brings you *Digital Photo* – the UK's best-selling photography and imaging magazine.

So, make sure you give this new way of learning a try because once you've been taught the *Digital Photo* way, you'll realise it's by far the quickest and easiest way to master Photoshop and Elements – and the best way to edit your images.

CLICK THE LOGO TO RETURN TO THE WELCOME PAGE
To leave any of the pages on our DVD, simply click on our logo to return to the welcome page.

NAVIGATION BUTTONS
You can easily find your way around the DVD by clicking on any of the four buttons at the top to load up the relevant pages.

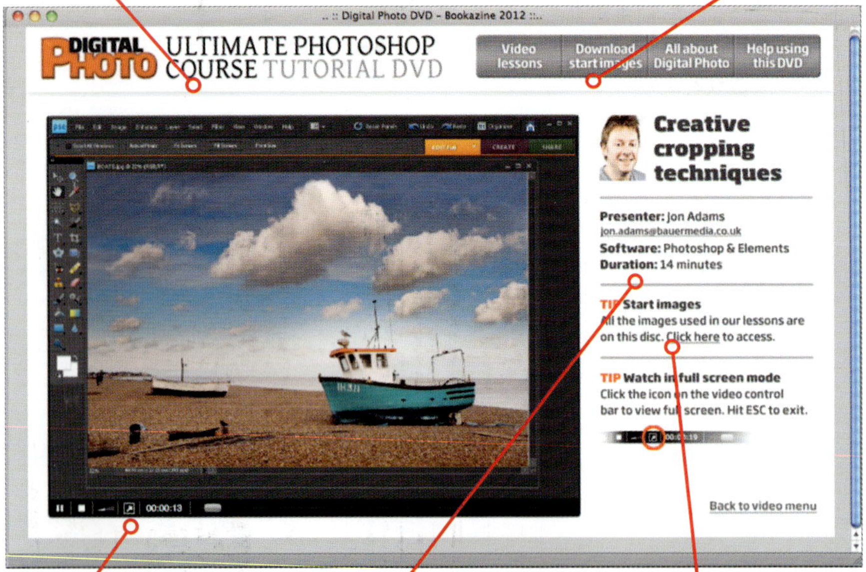

WATCH IN FULL SCREEN
Click on the arrow to view the tutorial full screen on your PC for maximum enjoyment!

VIDEO INFO
Find out the software needed and how long the video runs for.

START IMAGES
To try a technique using our start images, click here to download them to your PC.

MINIMUM SYSTEM REQUIREMENTS

PC USERS: Windows XP, Vista or Windows 7 with Internet Explorer 7 or later, the latest version of Adobe Flash Player (visit *www.adobe.com* and click *Flash Player* to check your system and download the latest updates) and a screen resolution of 1024x768 or higher.

MAC USERS: Mac OS X, Safari or Firefox, the latest version of Adobe Flash Player (visit *www.adobe.com* and click *Flash Player* to check your system and download the latest updates) and a screen resolution of 1024x768 or higher.

TROUBLESHOOTING

We've done everything possible to ensure that *Ultimate Photoshop Course* DVD and its accompanying video lessons will function perfectly on a wide range of different computers and in many different web browsers and media players.

TRY THIS FIRST

- **CD does not play?** Make sure you have a web browser installed such as Internet Explorer, Safari or Firefox.

Note: Using Google Chrome can cause problems running our videos, so try swapping to one of the above if the videos don't run.

- **Movies not running/visible?**

Check your browser (see above) and if videos still don't play, get the latest version of Flash Player from *http://get.adobe.com/flashplayer*

- Log on to *www.photoanswers.co.uk/cd* and follow the on-screen troubleshooting guide.
- **Can't copy start images?**

Navigate to the DVD via *Start*➔ *My Computer/Computer*, and drag & drop the *Start Images* folder onto your desktop.

- **Can't see all the movie?**

Click the *Full Screen* icon on the playback controls of the video. Hit *Esc* to return.

DAMAGED DVD

- If your *Ultimate Photoshop Course* DVD is damaged in some way, please return it to: *Digital Photo* DVD returns, Media House, Lynch Wood, Peterborough PE2 6EA.
- If you've visited the troubleshooting guide at *www.photoanswers.co.uk/cd*, read the tips above and are still having problems, e-mail us at: *dp@bauermedia.co.uk*. Please note that we can only assist in DVD related issues and are unable to help with computer problems.